Willow Working

by
Lynn Huggins-Cooper

PEN & SWORD
HISTORY
AN IMPRINT OF PEN & SWORD BOOKS LTD.
YORKSHIRE · PHILADELPHIA

First published in Great Britain in 2020 by
Pen & Sword History
An imprint of
Pen & Sword Books Ltd
Yorkshire – Philadelphia

ISBN 978 1 52672 460 1

A CIP catalogue record for this book is
available from the British Library.

Typeset in Ehrhardt 12/17 by
SJmagic DESIGN SERVICES, India.
Printed and bound in the UK by 4Edge Ltd, Essex, S55 4AD.

Pen & Sword Books Limited incorporates the imprints of Atlas, Archaeology,
Aviation, Discovery, Family History, Fiction, History, Maritime, Military,
Military Classics, Politics, Select, Transport, True Crime, Air World,
Frontline Publishing, Leo Cooper, Remember When, Seaforth Publishing,
The Praetorian Press, Wharncliffe Local History, Wharncliffe Transport,
Wharncliffe True Crime and White Owl.

For a complete list of Pen & Sword titles please contact

PEN & SWORD BOOKS LIMITED
47 Church Street, Barnsley, South Yorkshire, S70 2AS, England
E-mail: enquiries@pen-and-sword.co.uk
Website: www.pen-and-sword.co.uk

Or
PEN AND SWORD BOOKS
1950 Lawrence Rd, Havertown, PA 19083, USA
E-mail: Uspen-and-sword@casematepublishers.com
Website: www.penandswordbooks.com

Contents

Introduction to Heritage Crafts

Heritage crafts are a part of what makes us who we are: part of the glue that has held families and communities together for centuries. That jumper your nanna knitted – a heritage craft. The willow basket made by your auntie – a heritage craft. Grandpa's hand-turned pipe – again, a heritage craft. These traditional crafts have been carried out for centuries, often handed down through families with a child learning the craft at a parent's knee. Heritage crafts are those traditional crafts that are a part of the customs and cultural heritage of the areas where they begin. A heritage craft is:

'a practice which employs manual dexterity and skill and an understanding of traditional materials, design and techniques, and which has been practised for two or more successive generations'.

Radcliffe Red List of Endangered Crafts Report, Heritage Crafts Association 2017

Heritage crafts are in trouble. The Heritage Crafts Association commissioned research into endangered crafts, supported by The Radcliffe Trust (http://theradcliffetrust.org/). The results make sobering reading. Greta Bertram, Secretary of the Heritage Crafts Association who led the research said:

The Radcliffe Red List of Endangered Crafts is the first research of its kind in the UK. We're all familiar with the idea of a red list of endangered species, but this is the first time the methodology has been applied to our intangible craft heritage. While some crafts are indeed thriving, the research has shown that all crafts, and not just those identified as critically endangered, face a wide range of challenges to their long-term survival. When any craft is down to the last few makers it has to be considered at risk as an unpredicted twist of fate can come at any time.

Some of the heritage crafts identified in the report are teetering on the brink of disaster and could be lost during this generation. One hundred and sixty-nine crafts were surveyed and were allocated a status of currently viable, endangered, critically endangered or extinct. The survey team spoke to craft organisations and craftspeople, heritage professionals and funding bodies, as well as members of the public.

Four crafts surveyed were seen as already extinct, having been lost in the last ten years: riddle and sieve making, cricket ball making, gold beating and lacrosse stick making.

Ian Keys, Chair of the Heritage Crafts Association, said:

We would like to see the Government recognise the importance of traditional craft skills as part of our cultural heritage and take action to ensure they are passed on to the next generation. Craft skills today are in the same position that historic buildings were a hundred years ago – but we now recognise the importance of old buildings as part of our heritage, and it's time for us to join the rest of the world and recognise that these living cultural traditions are just as important and need safeguarding too.

An alarming seventeen more crafts are seen by the report as critically endangered and at serious risk. There are few artisans practising the crafts – sometimes there are just one or two businesses operating – and there are few or no trainees learning the craft anew as apprentices. So why do we find ourselves in this situation? At a time when a huge variety of crafts enjoyed as a hobby are booming, and craft fairs pop up in every community centre, village hall and historic estate, it seems odd that traditional crafts are dying out. So why is there a problem?

The study found that for some of the endangered crafts, there was an ageing workforce with nobody young training, waiting in the wings to take over. For others, there were found to be few training courses, even if there were potential trainees. For some traditional crafters, the problem was found to be a variety of economic factors. Cheap competing crafts from overseas have flooded the market and there is often an unwillingness of the part of the public to pay a fair price for items handmade in Britain, despite the craftsmanship involved and the high quality of products. Of course, most traditional craftspeople are running microbusinesses, and it is difficult to run a small business in Britain with an increase in paperwork, red tape, rules and regulations. Add to this the quantity of bureaucratic tasks and marketing necessary for self-employment, and that leaves scant time for honing and practising an artisanal craft.

The future of heritage crafts is threatened in Great Britain. Action needs to be taken now to reverse the trend and ensure that these heritage cultural traditions are not lost forever. So far, we are failing. Great Britain is one of only twenty-two countries out of one hundred and ninety-four to not have ratified the 2003 UNESCO Convention on the Safeguarding of Intangible Cultural Heritage. This convention focuses on the non-physical aspects of heritage such as traditional festivals, oral traditions, performing arts and the knowledge and skills to produce traditional crafts. If governmental action is not taken soon, many heritage crafts will be consigned to history.

You can help by supporting heritage craft workers with your wallet, and by attending demonstrations and events. You can also join the Heritage Crafts Association, even if you are not a heritage crafter yourself, to support the funding and research of heritage craft practices. At the time of writing, in 2019, it is £20 for an individual to join. (*http://heritagecrafts.org.uk/get-involved/*)

Chapter 1

Introduction to Basketry

Basketry is an ancient craft. Like many crafts it began as a response to a need – people needed containers and things to carry items in and they wove containers from plant materials that were readily available in their locale.

Baskets are part of the cultural heritage of most indigenous peoples around the globe, with an astonishing array of materials, styles and patterns being used. In Ancient Rome, willow was cultivated for basketry and there is evidence of basketry in Ancient Japanese and Chinese cultural traditions. Baskets seldom survive from antiquity as they are made from somewhat perishable materials. Fragments of the oldest baskets to have been discovered by archaeologists were found in Egypt and have been carbon dated to between 10,000 and 12,000 years old. Baskets found in the Middle East have been dated to around 7,000 years old.

Multi-purpose baskets developed around the globe, with different styles suiting the different materials used, from fine grasses to palms and bromeliads in more tropical climates. Basketry is woven from a wide variety of materials such as easily-dyed raffia (fibre processed from the raffia palm, native to Southeast Asia) and rattan, the leaves and stems from a tropical palm. Rattan is often referred to as wicker, or reed. It is durable, but harder to work with and needs to be soaked and woven damp. Plant fibres, including roots, canes, twigs, leaves, reeds, grasses and vines have been used to create basketware. Some were chosen for strength and pliability, others for decorative colour. Dogwood, larch, blackthorn, ivy, rose, privet, broom, clematis and chestnut have all been used, as well as rushes and willow. Wood is used in some designs and plant fibres are sometimes dyed for decorative purposes.

The fibre used to create a basket drives the character of the finished piece. Fibres may be round, flat, flexible or somewhat stiff. A basket designer often looks at the available fibres and designs a piece accordingly, to celebrate and enhance the fibres as the basketry is created. Willow has been the favoured material for centuries. In fact the Old Norse word for willow is *vikker*, which gives us the modern term 'wicker'. It is strong, yet pliable and puts on new growth quickly – up to 3 metres a year. Willows thrive in wet soil, and it has now been found to be an excellent plant for 'cleansing' soil of heavy metals and other toxins. Basket willow, or *Salix Viminalis*, takes up cadmium, lead, uranium, mercury, chromium, selenium and fossil fuel hydrocarbons.

Around the world, in simple economies, plant material for weaving into containers and baskets was gleaned from the hedgerows and forests, chosen for flexibility and strength. We tend to think of willow for baskets, but traditionally many other materials have been used. Tree wood was (and still is) split for use in weaving baskets, fences and hurdles. In England, these strips were known as *spale* or *spelk*, and in America, *splits* or *splint*. Many woodland areas were managed by coppicing and pollarding to provide materials to be woven. In coppicing, trees are cut to a low stump at ground level, to promote the growth of thin, pliable stems. In pollarding, the trees are cut to about 2 metres above ground to promote the growth of new stems for weaving; the height above ground is to protect the growth from grazing by wild animals such as deer or farmed sheep.

Many varieties of wood were utilised. Oak strips were used as warp and weft in weaving. Thin splints were used to weave baskets and containers for crops, such as punnets for valuable soft fruit. Sweet Chestnut was valuable weaving material; one-year shoots were woven like willow and older, thicker stems were used for rims and handles. Larger, older stems were split for stronger pieces such as hurdles and fences to keep domestic animals confined. It was highly rot resistant and long lasting. Hazel was used as it was flexible and naturally throws out multiple new stems as it grows which may be sustainably harvested. Ash, flexible and easily cleft, was woven into strong baskets.

In Scandinavian countries, pine has been split and used for basketry due to its widespread natural growth and availability. Spruce and juniper have also been commonly used, including the long and fibrous roots. Bark from trees such as birch and rowan have been chosen by weavers in northern countries.

Willow was first used from the wild, but cultivation has been carried out since Roman times. It was selectively bred for strength, straight wands, and pest and disease resistance. Willow is cut and soaked before weaving. It can be used 'in the green', straight after cutting, but the material does shrink as it dries. For this reason, most wands are 'seasoned' by keeping them for six to eight weeks before use. Rods cut in winter would be dried and then soaked before weaving to make them pliable. These were normally used with bark on and called brown willow to create containers or pieces that had to sit in water as the bark (or the tannins in the bark) resisted decay.

White rods could be created by cutting rods in spring before bud break and stripping the bark. Buff rods (the most usual) were created by cutting the willow wands in the dormant period between autumn leaf fall and spring bud break. These wands were boiled with bark on and then stripped and dried. The bark tannins stain the wood of the rods an attractive reddish brown and they are very pliable.

All willow rods, except those used in the green, require soaking before use. Brown takes from five to twenty-five days to become pliable again, as the water needs to penetrate the semi-waterproof bark. White or buff wands take a matter of hours soaking to be ready for use.

Grasses and cereal stems – as a by-product of food production – have also been widely used to make baskets and containers. Straw from crops such as barley, wheat, oats, corn and rye were collected after threshing (when the grains were removed from the stalk). The stems were combed into bundles and wrapped with strong, flexible plant material such as blackberry or willow strips. The bundles were then coiled into baskets. In coastal areas, tough marram grass was used; this was particularly true in the Orkney Islands and parts of Wales. For weaving bags and chair seats, rushes, reeds and cattails were employed. On the north-west coast of Britain, dock stems were woven into strong back baskets and heather was made into sturdy rustic lobster pots.

Tools such as awls, clippers, secateurs, planes, knives and hammers are used for basketry. Splitters and shavers prepare rods for weaving, and measure sticks and rulers are needed for making sure materials are the same size. Bodkins are used for piercing material and beaters for pushing the weave close together to make a tight, firm basket. Tubs are needed to soak materials and thick blunt tapestry needles if coiled and sewn baskets are created.

There are many construction methods in basketry:

- Coiling
- Plaiting
- Knotting
- Weaving
- Twining
- Looping
- Assembly
- Net
- Stake and strand

Coiling uses core material such as sedge, straw, rush, grass, sisal, jute, pine needles, willow, palmetto, sweet grass, yucca or leaves which are then bound into a thick strand with flexible material such as strips of bramble, skeined willow, raffia, horse hair, hazel or spruce. The materials are then coiled in a spiralling oval or round shape. A needle made from bone, metal or hardwood is used to pierce the coil and make gaps for stitching. To secure the layers of the basket as it grows, each coil is stitched to the previous coil. Coil baskets are normally round or oval, although other highly decorative shapes are made. Simple coiled baskets have historically been used for shallow domestic baskets and containers and also coiled skeps for bees.

Plaiting uses a woven pattern which in its simplest form has two sets of materials that cross each other, over and under, at right angles. The strips may be single, or bundles of material such as grass may be used. Plaited baskets may also be woven from slit sheet material such as birch bark.

Twining is where two or more flexible materials are used to encircle a base element. Highly decorative baskets can be made using this technique. Materials such as brush, waxed linen, elm bark and cordage feature in this type of basketry.

Weaving is used to create baskets with rigid materials creating stakes for the warp of the weaving with flexible materials woven in and out to create the weft. A myriad of materials is employed for this type of basketry with everything from wood and bark to willow and coiled paper. Splint weaving uses flat materials such as reed and cane, with peeled strips of oak, ash and hickory. Round-fibred weaving uses willow, honeysuckle, grape and hop vines – basically, any fibre that is flexible enough to be woven and strong enough to make a lasting basket that will stand up to the wear and tear of every day use.

There are a variety of basket weaves. Check weave, for example, is a basic flat weave suitable for square and angular basketry. Twill is similar, but the flexible material weaves over and under every second or third vertical stem. This creates a lovely diagonal pattern. Twinning is a tight weave that uses two horizontal threads that cross over between each vertical stem.

Looping and Knotting uses plant material that has been processed into two-ply cordage, a kind of fine twine. The technique has been known for centuries and the nets and baskets made have been used for gathering foods and foraging, as well as for fishing. The method can make bowls, bags, baskets, nets and sculptures. Modern artists use a range of plant materials to produce the twine, including phormium, iris, and daffodil leaves. Once the twine is created it is made into loops to make flat, two-dimensional 'fabric'; it can also be used to create three-dimensional pieces such as vessels, bags and pockets. Looping uses techniques such as increasing and decreasing the number of loops as work is carried out (a little like in knitting) and knots can be inserted to stabilise fabric, add texture and interest to a piece. Moulds can also be used with this technique, such as glass jars and board.

Stake and Strand was originally developed in the Roman era. The base is woven first, and stakes are either attached to the base or pushed into it. The material woven in to create the sides of the basket is known as the strand. Once the sides are woven, the stakes are used to form a border or rim. Traditional Scottish *crans* are made using the stake and strand method.

Today, baskets are still made by hand. It is interesting to see a craft that has not seen mechanisation on such a great scale as other artisanal crafts such as spinning, weaving or tanning. This has created a unique timeline in the development of the craft into the modern day, with highly skilled artisans still leading the field.

Baskets are cheap to make and have been made with a huge variety of materials in different locales. Down the ages, basketry has been used for a wide variety of things: footwear, carpets and floor coverings; as baby carriers, plates and cups; for catching fish, animal pens, harnesses, straining foods and drinks; for coracles to sail in – which were really giant waterproofed sailing baskets covered in hide – as well as sleeping mats and woven huts to live in. Wattle and daub housing was based on basketry techniques – a wooden frame was built and woven basketry panels or 'wattle' were added. The 'daub', a clay containing animal and human hair and dung, was added to the wattle and set hard like plaster or cement. These buildings lasted for centuries and were well insulated and warm.

In Roman times, wicker shields, chariot fronts, carts and shoes were made using basketry techniques for both cattle and horses suffering from tender hooves. Dry food and fruits and vegetables were gathered in baskets and liquids carried in waterproofed, tightly woven basketry. Water can be boiled in tightly woven baskets by adding hot stones. Basketry has been used to create shoes, sandals, clothes, hats, mats and carpets, as well as traps for hunting, hurdles for containing livestock for farmers, trays for winnowing cereal crops and special basket-nets for catching lobsters and salmon. Lobsters and crabs are still caught in basketry traps in some parts of the world today. As they swam downstream, eels were caught in rivers in specially woven wicker baskets called eel bucks. The baskets, mounted on frames which could be lowered and raised, were made from local willow, harvested on the banks of the rivers, especially on the Thames in the south east, where eels made up a large and nutritious part of the diet of the poor.

In England alone, there were hundreds of types of basket, each fulfilling different needs. For example, the herring trade utilised at least seven different types. Basketry was used at one point for trapping the fish, sorting them, as a receptacle for the ice needed to keep the fish fresh on its way to market and even for grading the fish according to government pricing. Right into the twentieth century, baskets were of huge practical importance in Britain, being used for everything from baby beds and carriages to carrier pigeon baskets and delivery carts for mail and foodstuff.

Baskets are still generally woven by hand today, mainly using plant fibres. They are used for utilitarian purposes – containing and carrying things – but may be ornamental in design. Today, baskets can be used to carry us on all parts of life's journey, from the 'Moses basket' (and perhaps the basket said to carry Moses downstream is the most famous basket in history) or woven crib, through to the woven caskets we can now be buried in. This green burial 'innovation' has of course been used before in history; Ancient Egyptians sometimes used baskets for burial (and indeed, made small *shabti* baskets to place inside the mummy case of the deceased – containing food to take the *shabti* figures through to the afterlife). Cave dwellers from cliff-based communities in ancient Arizona also followed this practice of placing bodies in basketware. It is interesting to note that the word coffin derives from the Greek *kophinos* which means basket. The link has been there for millennia.

Basketry has been such a mainstay of human development that is even included in Creation stories. Ancient Mesopotamians believed that the world began when a woven wicker raft was placed on the oceans and soil was spread upon it which made the land masses. A similar creation story from the Coos people from the south-west Oregon Pacific coast describes the land as created from five soot discs, a split-woven mat and a split-woven basket which were cast into the sea. In a Yakuma origin story, Woman prayed to a mythical being called *Saghalee Tyee* and was given skills or crafts, including basketry. A Navajo origin story talks of twins emerging onto the surface of the earth and learning to live on the surface. One twin made pottery from the clay of the earth and the other made baskets from plants such as reeds. A story from the tradition of the Pomo people describes the way *Marumda* taught women how to prepare materials for basket making and how to weave baskets and fishing nets. The Yuki people have an origin tale for the sun, where *On-coye-to* stole a bright light hanging up, stored it in a basket and returned to the world with it. He hung the sun in the far eastern sky but was not satisfied with the position. He repositioned it a little higher every day and still moves it across the sky to this day.

Vessels to carry the produce people grew and the food they produced from it, as well as for storage and transport of other goods they created and owned, have been part of human civilisation from earliest times. Without bags and baskets people could not hold, carry and transport the many things needed for everyday life. Basketry is not created for purely utilitarian purposes, however – it is, and has always been, an art form – even everyday baskets carry the story of the locale where they were made and the plant life that thrives there.

The variety of basketry around the world is endless, for all the similarities of method such as weaving. History and tradition can be read in the bend and turn of every basket. From the broad palm leaves of the tropics to the fine grasses of the savannah, plant material is woven to tell the stories of the societies and artisans that created them. As trade routes grew and travelled further afield, baskets tell the story as styles mingled. Migration took local traditions across the globe in a glorious crafting pollination of styles, traditions, methods, patterns and colours. Even dark times caused artisanal basketry styles to creep across the world – war and slavery contributed to the forced movement and settlement of peoples, and with them came their artisanal traditions. African slaves, ripped from their homes, brought skills of weaving and coiling baskets to their new countries and these styles cross-polinated with local traditions.

Even those 'useful' baskets have been often woven down the ages with the inclusion of symbolism, religious iconography and as ethnic and cultural icons.

There has been a massive decline in basket making in the UK from its heyday. Numbers began to fall in the nineteenth century: the 14,000 recorded in 1891 had dropped to 5,500 by the mid-1930s. Basketry suffered as new materials such as plastic were introduced as packaging for goods in the agricultural, domestic and industrial spheres. The Heritage Crafts Association now puts numbers at around 200. England once had around 10,000 acres of willow beds across the country in places such as the Somerset Levels. Place names such as Wythenshawe and Withy Grove in Manchester are the only remnants of once thriving willow production. There are now only around 300 acres of willow across the country being grown commercially for lengths of sallow, or *withies*.

Chapter 2

Ancient Basketry

Basketry has existed for nearly as long as there have been people on the earth. The oldest known baskets were found by archaeologists at Fayum, in Egypt. Carbon dating has found them to be from around 10,000 BC. Twined baskets dating back to 7,000 BC were discovered in Danger Cave in Utah, an area some archaeologists call Oasisamerica (the area defining pre-Columbian southwestern North America). Baskets made with interwoven methods date back to 3,000 BC and fragmented remains are fairly common.

It has been suggested that basketry even pre-dates cloth weaving, and furthermore, that the weaving of twigs, leaves and grasses led to the notion of weaving fibres into fabric. Basketry may even have been instrumental in the development of pottery. Curators at The British Museum have a 3,000-year-old complete basket on display. It has been suggested that baskets such as this were 'the mother of pottery' as potters used baskets as moulds to make vessels. Pieces of Neolithic pottery have the imprint of basketry, showing that the clay had been moulded and pressed against basketware to make bowls. Pottery shards from Gambols Cave in Kenya, dated at 8,000 BC, have basketwork impressions on their surface. Stone Age pots were also decorated with impressions from woven baskets. Some archaeologists have suggested that this imprinting was not as a result of using woven bowls as a mould, but rather a way of waterproofing them – an interesting theory.

It has even been suggested that pottery was 'invented' when baskets lined with clay for waterproofing were accidentally burned, and the baskets burned away leaving fine clay vessels.

Ancient willow remains are found at many dig sites; in the Brue Valley in Somerset, remnants of willow weaving was discovered as part of the excavation of a prehistoric wooden trackway. The remains of woven hurdles and baskets have also been found at an Iron Age site at the Glastonbury Lake Village site.

The problem for archaeologists is that woody and plant materials decay easily. They are mainly made up of cellulose, which softens as it decays and up to 80 per cent gets replaced by water. If the basket dries out again, it distorts and shrinks so archaeologists have to work onsite, often in waterlogged and boggy conditions, to draw and photograph the basket as it is. An example of this was a wicker creel made for fish found in the Shetland Isles which was dated to AD 337-607. Sometimes saturated baskets are preserved by using a 'wet box' which preserves the shape. Ancient basketry is of particular interest to archaeologists and historians, not just in itself, but also because of the story it tells by its construction. The materials and tools used and how any wood used was grown and cut can all tell a rich and complex story.

Ancient Eqyptian Basketry

Many of the ancient examples of basketry on display in museums around the world today are from Ancient Egypt. That is partly due to the fact that basketry rots quite readily over the years, with being biodegradable natural materials – and so are rare finds in many parts of the world. Yet in the dry atmosphere of Egypt, and due to often being packed into sand, many baskets or basketry fragments have been preserved for countless centuries. Basketry is found in the earliest Ancient Egyptian sites, with remains found dating from the Neolithic period, from around 5,000 BC. Apart from the remains, there are many images of basketry on Ancient Egyptian monuments and tombs.

In Ancient Egypt, many items were made using basketry techniques, from small baskets for produce and food up to larger objects such as furniture, weir baskets for fishing on the Nile and grain silos made from plaited reeds and coiled straw. Ancient Egyptians even made rafts from basketry-type techniques. By the time of the New Kingdom (between the sixteenth century BC and the eleventh century BC) the Ancient Egyptians were creating complex and beautiful basketware. In addition to baskets to hold food, they made and wove beautiful mats, fans, shoes and bags. Many objects were woven from a variety of plant fibres combined, and a range of weaving techniques were used. Fibres were plaited, bound and sewn and cordage was created for use in the design of objects.

Lightweight baskets and bags were used to carry dry goods such as corn and food, while builders used stronger ones to carry clay and raw materials. Foundry workers used baskets to carry charcoal. Many of the baskets were woven with reinforced handles and this strengthened them so they could be used to carry heavy loads. Storage baskets were often made using coiled methods and some had woven lids. Other baskets had attached cording and archaeologists have surmised that these were used to hang them from the roof or wall, presumably to keep food safe from rats.

Coiled, twined and plaited baskets were all made in Ancient Egypt. Baskets were made using date palm and doum palm leaves, which were plaited or used to wrap bundles for coiled baskets. Halfa grasses, flax, rushes and sedges were often twisted into cordage, to create twined baskets. The baskets sometimes used dyed materials in black, red and white and were often decorated with colourful stitching and even animal designs.

Rush matting was commonplace. Floors were hard surfaces, often made from stamped clay, and mats made the floors more comfortable as a place to sit. They were also used on beds and over doors and windows, as they could be rolled up when not in use. Mats were also used to decorate the walls and for roofing small, mud brick houses. Mats were even part of funeral practices; corpses were often laid out on mats and could be rolled in them.

Wooden storage chests were expensive and rare – wood was in itself a rare commodity due to the climate and lack of readily available trees in the natural environment. For most families in Ancient Egypt, baskets were the main storage system.

At Kahun, the archaeologist Petrie wrote in his journals (1888-1889) that he discovered a huge amount of basketware:

... a basket with beads and a bronze ring the set of copper chisels and hatchets, found in a basket which had contained a small alabaster jar, basket-work which had held the smaller things and rotted clothes. and most of the small objects were found in oval baskets of the Nubian type, with woven patterns on the sides, and a ridge lid. Small, flat, square baskets of rope were made, about 6 or 7 inches in height and width. And a band, probably for going round the back of a man in palm climbing, is formed of 14 fine ropes parallel, interwoven with strips of linen cloth, and ending in two thick loops for attaching the rope. Baskets were also made of palm leaf; both of the modern round type with palm rope handles, and of the flat, square form; the latter is most thoughtfully designed, with a wooden bottom bar, woven rope corners, six fine ropes up the sides to distribute the pressure, retained in place by a cross rope, and ending in a twisted rope handle, the top edge having a fine rope binding.

When Tutankhamun's temple was opened, rush-work chairs were discovered as well as a wealth of other basketry items. Eight baskets, all around 50 centimetres tall, were filled with doum fruits, a sweet orange fruit from the doum palm which grows as a native plant in southern Egypt. Also known as the gingerbread fruit, this food was often traditionally offered to mourners at funerals and was placed in the tomb to provision the pharaoh on his journey to the afterlife.

Ancient Roman and Greek Basketry

Basketry was widely used in the classical world. The *calanthus*, for example, was a basket popular in Ancient Greece, which looked a little like a top hat and was woven from reeds or thin twigs. It can be seen as a recurring image in ancient Greek art where it was a symbol of fertility and abundance. It was used to contain and carry things such as fruit or skeins of wool. In the Roman world, these types of baskets were used in agriculture, for harvesting fruit and other produce so it could be carried in from the fields. They used wild blackberry stems, split and dried as binding material for straw coil work. It has been said that the Romans prized willow more than corn, as they were used for so many purposes from chariot making to furniture and basketware. Fragments of Roman era willow and basketry have been found at many sites, such as the salt-making site on the River Huntspill on the Somerset Levels and the Iron Age settlement and Roman temple site at Marcham in Oxfordshire.

At Marcham, a large waterlogged pit from the Roman period was discovered and in 2006 a Roman pot and a worn shoe were found there. A basket was also discovered. The organic material had been preserved by the muddy, anaerobic conditions in the pit which was below the level of the water table. The basket was incredibly fragile and was moved for preservation, conservation and study to the York Archaeological Trust

Laboratory in a solid block of mud held in a container of water. At the laboratory it was painstakingly and slowly extracted from the mud and then the long process of conservation began. The basket was immersed in a wax solution for several months to strengthen and protect the delicate organic fibres. It was found that the basket was made from a kind of fine willow that is no longer cultivated in Britain – but Roman sources such as Pliny talk about fine willow being woven into contemporary baskets. Experts attempted to create a reconstructed replica of the basket, which was a difficult task considering that the base was gone and the material had been warped by the passing centuries. It is thought that the original basket was round and drum shaped, with a lid and possibly a handle.

Interestingly, it has been suggested that the twined basket was 'killed' in the same way as had other items in the pit. The pot, for example, had suffered a stab wound, perhaps from a spear. The base of the basket was sheared off by a blade. These items may have been ritual offerings, damaged so that they could no longer be used. The very fine weave suggests that the basket could have been specially made to carry precious objects, or sacred items. It may even have been a basket for sacred healing oils, like the similar basket found in the area of Roman Gaul which is now displayed in Cairo Museum. The temple at the Marcham site was associated with healing, so this may well have been the case, and the 'precious' basket would have been a fitting and highly valued sacrifice. We see baskets carried by priestesses in both ancient Roman and Greek texts, and baskets were used particularly in the worship of Demeter and Dionysus. The sacred basket of Demeter even appears on Greek coins.

The Americas

America has a long and beautiful tradition of basketry. Some archaeologists believe that the first people to colonise the Americas migrated across the Bering Strait – the land between Russia and modern-day North America – via a land bridge that existed at the time, called Beringia, around 11,000 years ago. The land bridge probably existed due to lower sea levels, which rose as glaciers began to melt. Other scholars believe that the first migrants came by sea, potentially 15,000-16,000 years ago. Jon Erlandson, an archaeologist from the University of Oregon, and Torben Rick, an anthropologist from The Smithsonian Museum of Natural History, talk of a 'kelp highway' which sea-going adventurers used to travel close to the coast along the southern edge of the Bering land bridge. The kelp would allow them to eat seafood and seaweed to sustain them as they travelled huge distances. This echoes the travel of migrants from mainland Asia to Australia that many anthropologists believe happened up to 45,000 years ago.

Historically, baskets were made from indigenous plants, as they were in most areas of the world. Human technology identifies a problem and responds to it using readily available materials. Grasses, willow and twigs were woven into often complex patterns.

Most groups of the First People developed basketry techniques that would grow and develop according to the materials readily available to them. In the Great Basin region, including Oregon, Nevada and Utah, many gorgeous examples of basketry have been discovered by archaeologists as they were preserved by the dry climate. Between 5,000 and 1,000 BC, people produced pottery moulded in baskets and the remains of these pots also tell us a lot about the patterns woven by early basket makers. Basketry was a multi-use artisanal skill that was not just utilised to create baskets to hold and cook goods (including tightly woven baskets to hold water and other liquids); it also created costumes for ceremonial use and for hunting. Baby carriers and cribs were made from basketry, often by men. Remains of nets and fish traps have been found, as well as woven snares for catching animals.

Each group of First People had their own methods, techniques, patterns and materials, creating an amazing array of basketry work.

In the north-west of America, the Tlingit and Chilkat people made fine, delicate baskets from twined plant fibre. In the north-east, baskets were often made from pounded ash and braided sweet grass fibre. On the north-western coast, baskets were made from swamp grass, spruce and cedar bark. In the south-west, the Apache and Hopi people created baskets from brightly dyed plant fibres, using geometric shapes to make coiled, highly patterned baskets; other groups made baskets from willow and sumac. In the south-east, the Cherokee people made traditional baskets from river cane – a type of wicker – and bundled pine needles. The Seminole people used long pine needles to create coils that were wrapped with grasses to be wound into baskets. In Canada, First People groups such as the Dene and Ojibwe people crafted beautiful, smooth baskets from birch bark.

A lot of traditional basketry was made from distinctive naturally coloured materials. Many dried materials were brown or beige, such as grasses and other plant fibre, and there were many shades of red material. Cherry bark, the inner bark of the cedar, red briar root, yucca root and California redbud were all used.

By the 1800s, the widespread settlements of white European migrants had driven the First People from much of their land. Their way of life and culture was largely destroyed as the result of systematic genocide and resettlement on reservations. In a sickening development, so called 'Indian' basketry became a popular decorating fad. Tourists would flood onto the Santa Fe Railroad and travel miles, buying collections of baskets. This was a highly fashionable thing to do, perhaps partly as a result of the influence of the Arts and Crafts Movement (1880-1920), which reacted to the growth of mechanisation and industrially-produced goods by bringing all things 'hand-made' into vogue as highly desirable items.

Fashionable Americans would return home and build cabins, decorating them with 'native' baskets, rugs and traditional beadwork items. Some people created so-called 'Indian' rooms in their houses, festooned with traditionally made artwork and goods.

Sadly, traditional skills were being eroded and lost as First People were forced to live reservation life. Artisans were exploited to make profits for entrepreneurs. A horrifying example of this practice was carried out by a man called Abe Cohn from Nevada. He virtually kept a skilled weaver called Dat So La Lee captive so she would produce baskets for wealthy tourists. He built a small house for her behind his and provided her with food and clothing – but no wage. She had to produce baskets for Cohn to sell at his Emporium Company in Carson City. He often paraded her there as a kind of living exhibit, weaving for the amusement of tourists and customers. Cohn pushed weavers to change their designs, tailored to what he perceived as the desires of his customers, thus destroying the very authenticity those tourists craved.

In fact, by the late 1800s, there was such demand for traditional basketry that much production actually moved overseas and was outsourced in a stunning example of cultural appropriation. The United States at that time governed the Philippines, which had a long history and tradition of artisanal, hand-made basketry. It was also a source of cheap labour. The rural artisans of the Philippines already grew plant materials specifically to use in the weaving of baskets which were then transported into towns and cities to sell. North American money financed training programmes, which were set up to duplicate the basketry traditionally made by the First People whose way of life they had obliterated. It seems incredible that such beautiful creations were almost 'counterfeited' in the 1800s in much the same way as desirable goods are counterfeited in the present day. The market was there and it was lucrative – so the baskets were made in the Philippines and exported to the United States. Today, the Philippine Islands are still major producers of woven artisanal goods and baskets on a global scale. Baskets were even created out at sea on the great American whaling ships. In Nantucket, in the early 1800s, local First People made baskets from ash wood splints, stripping and soaking the wood and weaving them around a square bottom. By the middle of the century the waters were busy with whaling ships hunting the waters south of Nantucket for the great whales, hungry for their lucrative oil supplies. In 1856 the State of Massachusetts responded to the dangers of the busy waters by commissioning lightships to act as floating lighthouses. During the day, the ten-man crews had little to do and they began to weave rattan baskets of their own in the style of the local baskets. They incorporated the moulds used by basket makers from Southeast Asia – perhaps as a result of travel and trade due to the movement of the whaling ships across different oceans.

The lightship basket makers prepared wooden bases for the baskets on shore and took them aboard to weave during the long days waiting to work the lightships upon the dark ocean. Tools were readily available on board, as the whalers carried coopers to make barrels for the whale oil. The Nantucket lightship baskets were useful around the house and sold well as a result. They must have sold well – in the early 1900s the government stopped crews from weaving baskets on board as they saw it as 'moonlighting' – a fine occupation for a lightship keeper! The baskets were so valued that owners would scratch the family name on the base or handle. To this day, although no longer made out on the open ocean, these baskets are still known as Nantucket lightship baskets. The skills of making these traditional baskets were passed down the generations and are still woven today, using oak, hickory and ash staves, with bottoms made from mahogany or pine. Interestingly, in the 1940s some of these baskets were adapted to make 'friendship baskets' with a distinctive

Nantucket carving on the top. It became a tradition for girls graduating from Nantucket High School to receive one of these baskets.

Today, thankfully, there has been a resurgence of traditional basketry made by First People artisans all over the United States, and artisans are celebrated for their skills. Natural plant materials such as galleta grass, yucca, cottonwood, sumac and cattail are still used to make stunning basketry to traditional patterns. Some materials are used in their natural colour; others are dyed with natural vegetable dyes in the same way as they have been made for thousands of years.

Chapter 3

Medieval Basketry

By the Middle Ages, although most housewives knew how to make a basket, it was common practice to trade goods with someone who actually specialised in making basketry items. These baskets were needed as containers for all manner of household necessities and were an important part of any household. They could be made from willow, vines, split wood or bark ribbons which were soaked to make them pliable. Basket weavers were often gypsies. Basketry was one of the few artisanal trades open to women.

One of Britain's first Christian churches, at Glastonbury, was roofed with straw supported by a wicker-work frame. The first monastery at Iona in Scotland, founded in 563AD by St Columba, was made from woven wicker. An early writer, chronicling the developments at Iona wrote of the monks being sent out *'to gather twigs to build their hospice'*.

Building with woven wood and other plant materials was massively important in the Medieval period. Woven sticks and wood were used by peasants to make their dwellings, which had thatched roofs, and walls of wattle and daub, a common building material. Wattles were panels woven from locally available coppiced wood, such as hazel, willow and ash. Split beech, oak or chestnut was also used and materials depended on availability locally and the status and wealth of the home owner. Daub was then plastered onto both sides of the wattle panel. It was made from subsoil, animal dung, chopped straw or grasses and water. The straw and dung (largely plant material) helped to bind the mix and stabilise and strengthen the clay, rather like modern clay strengthened with fibres. Local aggregates were also added to the mix for durability and to control shrinkage as the daub dried. This could include sand, fine gravel or chalk. The mix had to be soft enough to pack into the weave of the wattle panel, but not too wet because a wet mix would shrink more as it dried.

Daub was mixed by treading (much like clay is in cob building methods) and this was often carried out by groups of people who stomped and mixed with their feet as they chanted and danced. It has also been suggested that animals were passed backwards and forwards over the mix to trample it.

In East Sussex, examples of decorated wattle and daub have been discovered by archaeologists. It is thought that decoration was widespread in Medieval times but for some reason less so as we move into the Tudor period, when wattle and daub was still used widely in the building of timber-framed houses. Patterns such as vertical wavy and straight alternating bands were believed to be fairly commonplace. A sample of daub from Talbot House, in Sellinge, Kent depicts an almost life-sized human figure.

Between the fourteenth and sixteenth centuries, basket makers' guilds were created in cities across Europe. Edward III encouraged foreign artisans to settle in London, but by the time Edward IV was on the throne, some restrictions were in place. By an Order of Common Council in 1463, foreign artisans, including basket makers, were only allowed to settle in an area of London called Blanche Appleton, a manor in the parish of St Katherine Coleman in Aldgate Ward – a place set aside for 'aliens'.

Basket making endured, despite the challenge felt by local basket makers of migrant artisans working in the industry, as baskets were still very much needed in all walks of life, and for many uses.

Chapter 4

Tudor and Stuart Basketry

The ghettoization of foreign nationals into Blanche Appleton that began in the medieval era meant that by Henry VIII's reign, when tensions rose and apprentices rioted in protest against foreign workers and illegal imports of artisan goods (such as basketry from Holland), the immigrant basket makers were easy targets. In 1517 apprentices marched on the area and attacked the homes and businesses of the foreign workers. This violent protest, referred to as 'Evil May Day', was the result of a series of inflammatory xenophobic speeches given in London. According to contemporary chronicler Edward Hall, a broker named John Lincoln commissioned Dr Bell to give a speech at St Paul's Cross on a busy and crowded Easter Saturday. In the speech, Bell called upon *'Englishmen to cherish and defend themselves, and to hurt and grieve aliens for the common weal.'*

A few hours later around a thousand apprentices had gathered on Cheapside. They somehow managed to free a number of prisoners incarcerated for attacks on foreign nationals and marched on an area around St Paul's Cathedral where many immigrants lived. Despite attempts to disperse them, an attack ensued and this led to windows and doors being broken, houses being looted and immigrant workers being beaten viciously. The Duke of Norfolk along with 1,300 soldiers routed the insurgents and by 3am they had supressed the riot. Three hundred apprentices were arrested but later pardoned as a result of Catherine of Aragon's pleading their case to her husband (it is said for the sake of their wives and children) after an audience in Westminster Hall. Thirteen rioters were convicted of treason and they were executed on 4 May. John Lincoln was executed three days later. By 5 May there were 5,000 troops in London to keep the peace.

Things settled for a while, but John Stow reports in his *Survey of London* that in 1538 a disastrous fire broke out among the basket makers in St Margaret Pattens Parish. The fire raged and more than a dozen houses were razed to the ground. Nine people died and the cause of the fire was seen (rightly or wrongly) to have been the negligence of the basket makers and their combustible raw materials. As a result, the Common Council ordered the community of immigrant basket makers to leave the city. They petitioned King Henry, but in 1541 he allowed the Common Council to enforce their eviction from the City of London.

In 1569 basket weavers in England were granted their own guild. On 22 September The Worshipful Company of Basketmakers was established by order of the Court of Aldermen. The basketmakers were accustomed to joining the Butcher's Company and were in this way permitted to practise their trade within the walls of the city. Butchers used baskets extensively and this may be why they joined this company. Basketmakers also joined the Turners' Company, again turners would regularly use and sell baskets. In the light of the terrible fire of 1538, it is interesting and somewhat foreshadowing to know that Pudding Lane was largely inhabited by basketmakers as well as joiners, butchers – and the bakers often blamed for starting the Great Fire of London in 1666.

In 1660 the guild tried to obtain a Royal Charter from the crown, but despite repeat applications in 1682, 1685 and 1698, nothing came of it. Incredibly, a Royal Charter was not granted until 1937, by King George VI.

Henry VIII's warship the *Mary Rose*, which sank off Portsmouth Sound in 1545, has been a treasure trove for archaeologists and historians, providing a window into the Tudor world. A wicker-covered wine flask, probably from the Beauvais region of France, was found. It is thought that the wicker had a practical rather than a purely decorative function; the bottom was conical, which may mean it was designed to stay upright on deck. Strong, sweet wine was only for the consumption of officers; the crew were provided with beer, which was seen as safer than water as the brewing process killed most germs. Water quality at the time was very poor, even though people did not yet understand why.

Chapter 5

Georgian Era Basketry

The Industrial Revolution, between 1760 and 1840, created a huge demand for baskets for packaging and deliveries. Trade was changing forever, as factories grew and overtook the home production and self-sufficiency of everyday life. Goods were increasingly produced centrally, in factories, and needed to be carried safely to their point of sale and onward to customers. Vast quantities of willows were planted and grown for basketry and baskets were made to standard patterns in the factories for packaging by businesses. Basket making became specialised and professional, and these basket weavers served long apprenticeships (five to seven years) becoming proficient at many techniques and methods of basket weaving.

The Georgian era ushered in the golden age of shopping – and shoppers needed baskets to carry their purchases. There was an explosion of development in large towns across Britain at this time, with streets – and even pavements – being widened to make access to shops and businesses possible. Previously narrow, dark streets became light and airy, and the hazards of mud and the filth from passing coaches were just a memory. The shopping experience became a pleasurable, sociable pastime where browsing ornate shop displays, as well as spending, became a recreational activity. Larger stores sprang up, staffed by polite and elegant shop assistants to cater for their customers' every need.

Elegant and exclusive shops were built in expensive urban locations for the wealthy to frequent, such as The Strand and Piccadilly in London, and in spa towns such as Bath and Harrogate. Even less wealthy areas began to burgeon with shops as well as traditional markets and this growth in commerce created a centre of social interaction in towns across the country. Without baskets to transport goods from the provinces, baskets to display items and baskets for transporting and delivering purchased items, commerce might have ground to a halt!

Street traders and door to door sellers plied their trade widely in the Georgian era, carrying goods to their customers in baskets and trugs across cities and towns. Hawkers and peddlers were found in busy places such as at major landmarks and wherever people gathered. They also stood on street corners, calling out to passers-by. This type of selling required baskets for the goods to be kept, displayed and transported. Men, women and children worked as peddlers, selling a wide variety of goods from household and decorative items to food. Some even sold ready-to-eat food in the same way as 'fast food' is sold today. Baked apples, chestnuts, pies, gingerbread cakes and more were sold to be eaten warm in the streets from traders using warmed pans of coals.

Hawkers would cry their wares so that passers-by would notice them. Rhyming cries such as '*Fair Seville oranges; fine lemons fine; round sound and tender, inside and rine*' were part of the sounds of the city and many less theatrical cries such as '*Four for sixpence, herring*' were heard ringing out across towns and cities. They were seen as a colourful part of city life, with characters such as 'The Turk' selling a health remedy (medicinal rhubarb) in the area around Russell Square in London for many years. Illustrated booklets about hawkers and their advertising cries were produced and distributed.

During the Georgian period, wealthy people entertained at lavish dinner parties. Special baskets woven from fine china clay and silver wire began to be used as decorative serving dishes at the table. Displaying these items was a status symbol and showed the wealth of the hosts.

Baskets of food such as bread, fruit and sweetmeats adorned the tables of the rich and could be passed amongst guests by using their ornate handles.

In the Regency period, from c.1795 to 1837, there was an explosion in building with characteristic ornate Regency decorations. Baskets were widely used on building sites at this time to move materials and mouldings. They could be made to any required shape and size and were light but strong. They were resilient when knocked and absorbed shocks so that often delicate plasterwork and moulding was not damaged. These baskets were mainly made from willow but could also be made from cane or rushes. Baskets were also used to transport goods from the manufacturers of building components and could be hauled directly up and down scaffolding. If you are ever lucky enough to visit Brighton in Sussex, look up and imagine all of those mouldings and curlicues being hauled up scaffolding in baskets. It makes the workmanship even more amazing!

Chapter 6

Victorian Basketry

The production of standardised basketry in factories for packaging, begun in the Georgian Era, continued apace in Victorian times. Willow also became a staple in the furniture industry at this time, with high demand for fashionable wicker furniture. Great tracts of willow bed were planted, not only in the Somerset wetlands as was traditional, but also further afield. At the beginning of the nineteenth century, more than 3,000 acres of willows were planted commercially in Dorset and Somerset in the southwest of England, around the River Parrett and its tributaries, the Isle and the Tone. Local farmers around the Somerset Levels – and many other landowners and entrepreneurs – rushed to make a profit and planted hundreds of smaller scale willow beds and soon there were hundreds of growers and suppliers, as well as basketmakers and furniture makers on the levels and moors. The wetlands were the natural habitat for *salix viminalis*, the common osier, *salix triandra*, or almond leaved willow and *salix purpurea*, the bitter or purple willow – the willows particularly favoured by basketmakers for strength, flexibility and vitality.

Industrialisation, and the large scale movement of trade and populations to urban areas could not have happened without the rise of the railways, and the railways needed willow hampers and chests to bring goods from rural areas to feed the workers. Items made in the burgeoning factories were moved by the railways and ultimately exported by sea – and that required large numbers of containers, often made from willow. Willow was used throughout society and in most industries. Willow items were eagerly bought by the hotel trade in London, as well as the catering trade, factories across the country who needed packaging and the new Post Office. The fishing trade, bakers, butchers and farmers and fruit growers snapped up basketry containers to get their supplies to market.

Highly specialised baskets were created for use by servants in grand houses, such as baskets with specially woven, cut out sides to accommodate plates that servants would have to carry for long distances through the household. Willow was also in great demand for the wicker furniture fashionable in the Victorian era. Similar styles are still used today in up-market picnic sets.

Basketry was even used as a therapeutic art in the Victorian era. The asylum system of the nineteenth century used 'recreational crafting' to occupy and soothe hospital and clinic inmates. The basketry was also sold to create an income. This continued from its beginning in the 1840s right up until the 1960s when the great mental hospitals began to close and the system changed. Occupational therapy today may still use basketry techniques to work with patients who need exercise to keep hand joints supple and flexible.

I am having unmistakable evidences, that what we have been doing for the occupation and amusement of our patients is becoming known very generally, and in many quarters, that are important to our permanent success, is recognized as a proof that we are at least in the front rank of [mental] *institutions.'*

1864 – Dr Thomas Kirkbride,
Pennsylvania Hospital for the Insane

Peddlers and hawkers still sold goods in the streets, the same as they had in the Georgian era. In Henry Mayhew's book *London Labour and the London Poor* he describes a wide variety of sellers and peddlers.

Some made a good living; others barely scraped by with the things they sold on the streets from their baskets. He described a man paralysed in one leg who worked selling groundsel and chickweed in Saffron Hill. He gathered the greens to sell to people who kept canaries and finches, a popular city pet. He collected the plants early in the morning and put them into bundles that he sold for a half penny. He then walked the streets with his basket of greens in different areas each day – for ten hours a day – to make money for his family. His wife was an out-worker, making braces but receiving only one shilling for every four dozen.

In 1861, Henry Mayhew wrote *The London Street-Folk comprising: Street Sellers, Street Buyers, Street Finders, Street Performers, Street Artisans and Street Labourers* about the markets and street hawkers of the day, who sold their wares from great baskets.

The pavement and the road are crowded with purchasers and street-sellers. The housewife in her thick shawl, with the market-basket on her arm, walks slowly on, stopping now to look at the stall of caps, and now to cheapen a bunch of greens. Little boys, holding three or four onions in their hand, creep between the people, wriggling their way through every interstice, and asking for custom in whining tones, as if seeking charity. Then the tumult of the thousand different cries of the eager dealers, all shouting at the top of their voices, at one and the same time, is almost bewildering. 'So-old again,' roars one. 'Chestnuts all 'ot, a penny a score,' bawls another. 'An 'aypenny a skin, blacking,' squeaks a boy. 'Buy, buy, buy, buy, buy— bu-u-uy!' cries the butcher. 'Half-quire of paper for a penny,' bellows the street stationer. 'An 'aypenny a lot ing-uns.' 'Twopence a pound grapes.' 'Three a penny Yarmouth bloaters.' 'Who'll buy a bonnet for fourpence?' 'Pick 'em out cheap here! three pair for a halfpenny, bootlaces.' 'Now's your time! beautiful whelks, a penny a lot.'

'Here's ha'p'orths,' shouts the perambulating confectioner. 'Come and look at 'em! here's toasters!' bellows one with a Yarmouth bloater stuck on a toasting-fork. 'Penny a lot, fine russets,' calls the apple woman: and so the Babel goes on.

So, in the nineteenth century basketmaking was an integral part of the supply chain for industry, carrying goods from the factories to the customers. At its peak, there were 14,000 basket makers in England alone. A tiny town in Manchester could have 200 basket makers, all working hard to supply the factories producing goods for shipping across the empire. Baskets themselves could not be made by the machines that filled the factories, and artisans worked flat out to provide the baskets needed by the hungry factories.

Furniture

Wicker furniture has been woven for centuries, with remains being found in the Ancient Egyptian and Roman eras and being made around the world ever since. A woven cane bed was buried with Tutankhamun in 1,323BC, and a cane coffin dating from 750AD was found in a Moche princess's tomb in Peru. Humans are adaptable creatures and have always used locally grown and gathered materials to make furniture. Wicker is the term used to describe weaving carried out using rattan, cane, willow and raffia. The materials are usually cut into strips and dried, before soaking again to make it pliable.

Cane was used throughout Asia, where the materials to make the furniture grew naturally, and it came to Europe due to trade. In the 1660s cane furniture appeared in Holland, England and France due to bustling trade with Asia. The chairs made were popular due to the way they were light and easy to clean, resistant to moths and dust. Interiors were not the cleanest or most hygienic at the time! By the seventeenth century, wicker furniture in Northern Europe began to look the way it does today, and was widely used for infant and baby furniture, such as cribs and bassinets, as well as for special furniture such as high-backed chairs for the infirm and elderly. The material was regarded as healthy and breathable and was, of course, softer and more comfortable (as well as cheaper to produce) than heavy wooden furniture.

Cane manufacturers sprang up in Europe and became popular in the highest circles. In the late 1780s, Marie-Antoinette's hair and make-up were attended to as she sat in a wicker chair. In England, Buckinghamshire was the traditional place for the manufacture of wicker and cane chairs.

In the Victorian era wicker was highly fashionable. No doubt prompted by the growth and strength of the British Empire, wicker furniture captivated the Victorians with its air of 'exotic' life in the colonies. Rattan was widely used in tropical countries as the materials it was made from were easy to obtain, and once made, the furniture did not warp, crack or easily rot in the humid, hot atmosphere.

As the nineteenth century wore on, wicker was used to create rather complex patterns with the curlicues and flourishes beloved of the time. Cane was used for the seats of many chairs, particularly 'café style' chairs which made them lighter and cheaper to produce in quantity. By the mid nineteenth century, wicker had travelled to America, where it was industrialised and mass-produced.

The companies of Wakefield and Heywood competed to invent newer, more efficient and cheaper production methods with machinery. Cyrus Wakefield had begun creating rattan furniture in the 1850s, using rattan that was used in ships as ballast and then unloaded at the destination port. Eventually, as his designs became popular, he began to import the material himself. The Heywood Chair Manufacturing Company invented a mechanical process to weave wicker seats. Eventually the two companies merged to become Heywood-Wakefield of Gardner,

Massachusetts, feeding the growing American market, developing and adapting to suit the tastes of their customer base. Over time, they moved from ornate Victorian designs to simpler styles such as Arts and Crafts and Art Deco styles.

As the twentieth century dawned, the demand for woven furniture was still large. In 1907 American Marshall Burns Lloyd revolutionised the production of woven furniture by creating a specialist loom that could twist a special paper and steel wire material. It claimed to be resistant to damp and dirt and was smooth to touch. There were none of the rough portions that were familiar with cane furniture, that could snag and pucker material and cause runs in fabric. This new substitute wicker was strong, durable and did not easily distort or break. This woven fabric became known as Lloyd Loom and it is popular to the present day.

In England, William Lusty was a manufacturer of packing crates. During the First World War they expanded business and made munitions cases. By the end of the war, the company was looking for a new line of products. When an agent introduced Lusty to Lloyd's new system of creating synthetic wicker, he acted quickly. He travelled to America in 1920 and spent time observing the process and working in the factory to familiarise himself with it. In 1921 be bought patent rights and machinery, and by 1922 the factory was in production on a 17-acre site in London, at Bromley-by-Bow. The area was close to the railway and the Limehouse Cut, a tributary of the Grand Union Canal. Its workers lived nearby in densely populated terraces of houses.

By the 1930s, Lloyd Loom furniture was wildly popular. Hotels, restaurants and the ocean liners all sported its smart, easy to clean and fashionable furniture in a range of colours. By 1940, an amazing ten million pieces of Lloyd Loom had been produced in the UK and America. During the 1950s onwards, demand waned as more 'modern' styles of furniture made from new materials such as plastic and Formica flooded the market. However, by the 1990s, Lloyd Loom was back and its furniture is still in production today. Lloyd Loom pieces are durable indeed – many pieces may be found at auction and in antique shops nearly a century later. They are easily revamped and with a lick of paint are upcycled ready to take their place in contemporary homes.

Most Lloyd Loom furniture is now made in the far east, in China, Vietnam and Indonesia, and only on a small scale in the United Kingdom.

Fashion

For centuries, willow hoops and basketry structures were a part of women's fashion. In the sixteenth century, for example, women wore a skirt supported by a frame. It was called a farthingale. This Tudor period hoop skirt was an undergarment that held fabric in a fashionable shape. The hoop first developed as a way to keep the skirt clear of the legs during activities such as gardening and later became a fashion item. On a practical level, the frame held heavy fabric away from the legs, so the wearer did not trip and also kept wearer cool in hot climates.

The farthingale originated in Spain and was originally woven from Giant Cane. The name *verdugado*, from which the word *farthingale* was derived, from the Spanish word *verdugo*, meaning *green wood*. Joan of Portugal wore *verdugado* in Spain, and the court followed suit, creating the fashion for farthingales. Catherine of Aragon wore the farthingale and brought it to England when she married Arthur, Prince of Wales in 1501. The English court subsequently adopted the fashion. In England, most farthingale hoops were made from osiers, or willow withies – and later, also whalebone. The fashion remained popular with the rather conservative Spanish court into the seventeenth century.

The French, or wheel, farthingale developed at the French court and was introduced to England by Anne Boleyn in the 1570s. It contained rolls of buckram and canvas, stiffened with reeds. This developed into the *great farthingale* of the 1590s, beloved of the court of Elizabeth I, which shaped the extravagant skirts we see in portraits of the queen.

In the 1600s, panniers or 'false hips' became popular. They were worn to extend the width of skirts at the side, creating a strangely squared silhouette. The word *pannier* comes from *panniers*, the name for baskets worn slung either side of a pack animal. The front and back of the skirt were mainly flat. Ornate embroidery and woven patterns were displayed on the pannier. We can see examples of the skirt style in portraits of the Spanish court by Velázquez. From Spain, the fashion spread to the French court and arrived in England in c.1710. These framed skirts were popular in various incarnations throughout the seventeenth century. By the mid eighteenth century, fashionable women could take up three times the width of a man due to the elaborate frame inside her skirts! By the 1780s, panniers were only really worn at court.

In the 1800s crinolines became popular. These full skirts were at first padded and made with horse hair (or 'crin') and one can only imagine the weight, itchiness and heat of such a garment. Thankfully for fashionistas of the time, these were replaced in the 1850s by crinoline frames made from wicker, gutta-percha (a type of rubbery sap produced by a tropical tree), willow, wire and whalebone. Some crinolines reached the dizzying circumference of up to 5½ metres! These dresses could be a hazard to the health of the wearer, however, and there are many records of the hoops getting caught in machinery, carriage wheels – or catching fire. Astoundingly, many women died but the fashion persisted. During the decade from the late 1850s to the late 1860s, close to 3,000 women in England died as a result of crinoline-related fires.

The Times newspaper on 13 February 1863 reported the death of a 14-year-old kitchen maid called Margaret Davey. She died when her skirt, stretched around a crinoline frame, caught fire at the hearth as she reached for spoons on the mantelpiece. The poor girl died from burns.

The Deputy Coroner passed a verdict of 'Accidental death by fire, caused through crinoline' and reported that he was: *Astonished to think that the mortality from such a fashion was not brought more conspicuously under the notice of the Registrar General.'*

By the 1870s, the smaller *crinolette* and the bustle had replaced the huge crinoline skirts. By the mid-1880s, the bustle had reached shelf-like proportions. This led to an amazing development, all made possible by the wonders of basketry. The *Derby Daily Telegraph* reported on the bustle with a 'living dress improver' in 1887 – where some fashionable ladies used the bustle shelf as a place to strap on a satin-lined cat basket! These were first seen in Luchon in the French Pyrenees, where the paper reported a cat-loving lady with a cat basket strapped to her bustle so she had her hands free to collect wildflowers.

A little basket padded and lined with satin and decked with ribbons to harmonise with the wearer's costume, serves as a cradle for the furry pet, and is just large enough when closed to contain his body, with a hole cut to allow the egress of his head. The basket is fitted with strings and tied around the lady's waist...

The cat bustle-basket was an instant and huge hit and spread quickly to fashionable ladies holidaying in France. *The Truth* reported in 1887 that the baskets were even seen at the sanctuary at Lourdes, with ladies being seen sporting *'a mountain tom or tabby on the dorsal hump'*.

So, basketry has been used for fashion as well as creating baskets, bags and cases. It has been used to weave baskets for pets – and even baskets to be worn, cats and all!

Any baby would sleep well in this wonderful Moses basket from Eddie Glew Basketry'.

This sturdy hamper was artfully created by Eddie Glew Basketry.

Alex Prain took this wonderful shot of Eddie Glews working with willow in the grounds at Wallington.

An amusing sketch from Punch Magazine in 1870, showing ladies with bustles as stately but laden snails.

 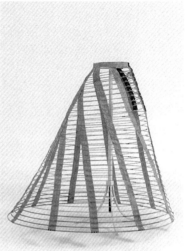

Above left: A glorious juxtaposition of wood and fibre in this piece by Colette Davies.

Above right: A huge crinoline underskirt support woven from willow and exhibited at MoMu, Fashion Museum of Antwerp. (Photo by Hugo Maertens)

This lovely basket was created by Eddie Glew Baskets at Blithfield Willowcrafts.

Eddie Glew, artisan willow worker.

Eddie Glew with a stunning willow sculpture.

Eddie Glew working 'in the field,' creating sculptures from willow in situ.

Stack of sturdily beautiful baskets from Eddie Glew Basketry.

Beautiful baskets from Blithfield Willowcrafts.

Above left: The natural hues of the materials, and the lovely pattern make this basket from Eddie Glew Basketry a piece if art.

Above right: Gorgeous woven case from Blithfield Willowcrafts.

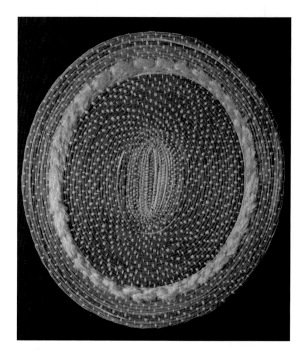

Exquisitely woven mat by Mae Adams.

This lovely textural piece by Mae Adams begs to be stroked.

Chapter 7

Twentieth Century Basketry

U p until around a hundred years ago, most villages had a basket weaver, as basketry was still such an important part of everyday life. Old maps from around this time may still have withy beds, where the willow was grown, marked upon them.

As the twentieth century dawned, large scale commercially produced baskets became more standardised and in 1916 the British Amalgamated Union listed precise measurements and quantity of willow to be used for particular basketry items, such as homing pigeon baskets, bath chairs for invalids, sieves, bread trays, linen baskets, hawker's baskets, pheasant hampers, plate baskets, bicycle crates, scuttles and wool skeps. Royal Mail even employed its own basket makers to make hampers for postal movement around the country.

In late nineteenth and early twentieth century Scotland, basketry was at the centre of the fishing industry. Apart from using baskets within the community in general, Scottish fisher-folk used a variety of basketry to establish commercial fishing, for example, baited traps or creels woven from willow to catch fish and trap crustaceans. They also used long lining – a type of line fishing – to catch fish such as halibut, ling, cod and flat fish. In small line fishing, the lines could be up to a mile long. Short lines were attached to this long line, and these held an attached hook. Women and children would bait these hooks with shellfish such as mussels that were collected on the shoreline. There were around 1,200 hooks per line, so this was a long and arduous task. The lines were kept coiled in specially woven baskets called sculls, to stop them from tangling. These baskets were oval with a lower front edge. In the Arbroath area, long flat sculls were used. In Portnockie sculls were deeper and smaller; in Dunbar and North Berwick, sculls had a curved rim.

Great line fishing was done in deep waters and the great lines were up to 15 miles long. They could hold up to 5,000 hooks which the fishermen baited on the boat. Fishing grounds could be as far away as the Faroe Banks north of Shetland. The sculls were larger than those used for small line fishing and had cork or rope around the rim to store the hooks.

Fishermen also used drift fishing with huge nets to catch the plentiful herring from May to November. The boats tracked the shoals around the Hebrides and the Northern Isles and down the east coast. The herring catch was measured in *crans* which equates to 1,000 herring. The fleets used quarter *cran* baskets to land their catch and measure it. These baskets were made to a regulation size and the Fishery Board for Scotland inspected regularly to ensure that measures were accurate. By the 1940s fish began to be packed in boxes and the baskets were used less.

In the Highlands of Scotland and down the east coast, great baskets called *creels* were used by both people and ponies to carry fish, and also peat, seaweed and heavy vegetables such as potatoes. They were generally woven from willow or heather and were made by sticking stakes deep into the soil and weaving around them. The base would be made by curving and bending the stakes. At one point many crofts kept their own willow patches to be used to make creels and other basketry items. A strap was attached to the creels make the basket easier to carry.

Jean Terry, writing in 1913 of fishwives at Cullercoats, a fishing village on the Tyne, said:

The Cullercoats fishwife, with her cheerful weather-bronzed face, her
short jacket and ample skirts of blue flannel, and her heavily laden

'creel' of fish is not only appreciated by the brotherhood of brush and
pencil, but is one of the notable sights of the district.

There was even a song written about the *fish lasses* of Cullercoats by a
Geordie music hall entertainer called Ned Corvan which went:

Verse:
Aw's a Cullercoats fish-lass, se cozy an' free
Browt up in a cottage close on by the sea;
An' aw sell fine fresh fish ti poor an' ti rich--
Chorus:
Will ye buy, will ye buy, will ye buy maw fresh fish?

Fishwives undertook the back-breaking work of carrying the creels
full of fish, sometimes with another basket called a *cob, murlin* or *scull*
balanced on the top. These were incredibly heavy once loaded, weighing
up to 8 stone. It took two women to lift a loaded creel onto a woman's
back and some creels had a head strap to help support the weight. They
also carried arm creels to display a sample and carry a cutting board.
These fishwives would walk inland, heavily laden, to sell their wares.
They would have a list of customers to visit and there was often a queue
of people waiting. On the journey back they would fill the creels with
peat and kindling.

In the Arbroath area an oval basket called a *rip* was used, often worn
on the hip to bear the weight. The women would go from house to house
selling, as well as selling from the creels or stalls in markets. Once there
were railways and trams, many fishwives used those rather than walk
into towns. The last fishwives only put down their baskets finally in the
1970s. The fish lasses of Cullercoats have been immortalised, carrying
their creels, in a variety of great paintings from the artists' colony that

formed in Cullercoats in the 1800s. Robert Jobling's *When the Boats Come In/Morning on the Beach* is a fine example.

Fishwives were also featured in author Jack Common's autobiographical novel *Kiddar's Luck* which describes Edwardian-era Tyneside. He talks of the fishwives walking down the back lanes of Heaton, a suburb of Newcastle:

> *Down here came the Cullercoats fishwives crying 'Caller Herrin' in that season and otherwise 'Fresh fish, hinny, straight from the sea'. They wore their traditional dress of dark blue which so well set off the biscuit tan of arm and face, the salt-white hair, and they were like caryatids walking under the great baskets they carried on the heads.*

In the First World War woven basketry cases were used to house shells that need to be kept safe from shocks, and woven willow hurdles were used to help to transport them across muddy ground between the trenches. Thousands of baskets were also used to transport the vitally important carrier pigeons, which carried messages backwards and forwards across the battlefields. Collapsible willow cages and woven backpacks were used to move birds. Willow was also used to make observational balloons, which rather heroically travelled across terrain to sight battle movements, and also required woven baskets to carry the observers. Pannier baskets were also used to move supplies and food to the troops.

In 1917 The National Society for the Promotion of Occupational Therapy was founded, and basket weaving was a mainstay of the approach of therapists working in the field. Photos of brave soldiers, wounded and returned from the front, were circulated and entered the public consciousness.

Harvesting willow was incredibly hard, back breaking and arduous work. Once harvested, the willow needed to be stripped of bark by hand.

Traditional basket makers worked with stripped willow which created a bright, strong finished product. Dried, harvested willow withies or strands were boiled in huge vats of water to soften them, and then pulled individually through a hand brake made from split wood or metal, to remove the bark. This boiled willow was an attractive ginger colour due to the tannins released by the bark. Freshly harvested willow cut in May could be stripped 'raw'. It was work mainly carried out by women and children. This would not change until the willow stripping machine was invented in the late 1920s. These machines could strip whole bundles of withies at once, but they were dangerous and injuries to the hands and fingers of operators were commonplace.

Until the 1920s, school children in Stoke St Gregory on the edge of the Somerset Levels were given their long holiday in May. The whole month was spent stripping willow for the Whitening Season, so-called because the raw willow was white when peeled and made high quality baskets. Willow was still often stripped like this by hand up until the 1950s.

During the Second World War the willow industry became vitally important. A Willow Officer was appointed, and a programme of research was undertaken at the Government Research Station at Long Ashton in Bristol. Virtually all willow was requisitioned by the Ministry of Defence and channelled towards the war effort, and the making of domestic baskets was banned. This does not sound important, but remember that at the time there were no plastic bags and people had to take their own bags to the shops to carry provisions. Many women were recruited to weave willow airborne panniers to drop supplies of food and ammunition to the troops on the front line. The flexibility of the willow allowed the panniers to be dropped from great heights without breaking. An amazing two million of these had been produced by D-Day.

Willow weaving was even used to help wounded and ex-servicemen to recuperate once they came home. Institutes for the Blind such as

St Dunstan's Hospital in Sussex were set up all over the country for ex-soldiers blinded by gas and injuries and basket weaving was seen as a great therapy and a way for blind people to learn a trade.

By the 1950s plastic had arrived as a cheap and desirable, versatile alternative to basketry containers and packaging. The methodical creativity of basketry has been seen as therapeutic, if not meditative (particularly in occupational therapy, for example). It is also popular as a mindfulness practice as part of the 'slow craft' movement. The industry went into decline and hundreds of acres of willow beds were lost. Things were looking dark for basket makers and willow workers, and there was a real danger that the skills passed down over generations would be lost forever.

Chapter 8

Modern Basketry

Whilst it seemed for some years that basketry would die out with the development of new materials and techniques, that has been far from the case. In fact, in the twenty-first century willow and basketry are seeing something of an upsurge. Green initiatives and the 're-use, recycle' movement has raised the profile of basketry and willow weaving in the search for natural, environmentally friendly products. The campaign against plastic as a result of concern about greenhouse gases and plastic waste in the oceans has led to mandatory charges for plastic bags in the United Kingdom as well as in other parts of the world, and this in turn has caused a growth in the market for reusable cloth bags and traditional shopping baskets. The growth of interest in sustainability as a way of life has resulted in the resurgence and development of carbon neutral production methods and basketry fits well into this ethos as it is hand-made and often uses locally sourced materials. Many basket makers grow their own renewable materials to use in the production of basketry, and basketry is of course woven by hand – and never by machine.

Green initiatives are seeing willow used in river *spiling* – a traditional method used in the modern world – which utilises the weaving of willow to reinforce river banks and preventing erosion. The technique, carried out in winter or early spring by weaving dormant willow withies, creates a natural willow retaining wall that can regenerate itself. Willow stakes are driven into the river bed and then are interwoven with living willow shoots which quickly establish and grow to create a dense root mass that stops the soil from being swept away by the action of the water. This type of bio-engineering can be woven into hurdles on site, with soil back-filled behind this new retaining wall, which in turn enables the live willow to root further and creates a stable bank. This traditional method was even described in a poem called 'The Land' by Rudyard Kipling, who spoke of the method thus:

They spiled along the water-course with trunks of willow-trees, And planks of elms behind 'em and immortal oaken knees.

Home gardening and landscaping has created a demand for rustic items such as woven fencing and hurdles, and flower and vegetable bed edging. Living willow is used to create domes, living fences and garden structures including play houses for children. Dormant, living willow stakes are driven into the ground and then woven into shapes that grow. These are maintained by weaving-in and clipping the growing willow each season.

Willow sculptures such as animals and birds for gardens are gaining in popularity, and there are many workshops available to help the arty gardener make their own simple sculptures. Large scale sculptures are also being created, such as the huge Willow Man created by willow artist Serena de la Hey beside the M5 motorway, near Bridgewater in Somerset. Willow mazes, such as the lovely Willow Orchid Maze designed by Charmian Marshall at The National Trust's Gibside Pleasure Garden, have also been woven by willow artists and artisans.

Basketry is now even growing in popularity in the green funeral market. Woven willow, abaca (a type of hemp fibre), bamboo, banana leaf, water hyacinth and seagrass coffins are now being made and are favoured by those desiring a 'greenfield burial' at many of the eco-friendly sites around the United Kingdom. They are also suitable for use in more traditional burials and cremations. Willow is still grown on the

Somerset Levels, as well as in other locations and it is possible to buy withies – willow rods – of many types and colours for projects as diverse as basket making and living sculpture building. Willow grows quickly, up to 8ft per year. New willow beds are established by planting slips of willow which sprout in the damp ground. Within three years they are mature and harvestable. Mature plants last up to 30 years of harvesting, and each give up to 30 withies each year. The crop is harvested when the leaves fall and the plant is dormant. Willow beds are also a great refuge for a diverse selection of wildlife.

Although machines are now used for cutting withies and stripping bark, the industry has not changed in many ways for centuries.

Chapter 9

Basketry in Ritual and Folklore

'Corn dollies' are made from the stalks of grass plants such as corn and barley. They come from an old traditional harvest custom, dating from Europe in the seventh century. The idea was that the spirit of the corn lived within the cornfield and when the corn was harvested, there was nowhere for the spirit to reside. The corn figure was often made as a symbol such as a Corn Mother or Maiden, or sometimes an animal. It was made as an embodiment or representation of the spirit and was kept throughout the year. By giving the Corn Spirit a home during the darkness of winter, the idea was that the spirit would look kindly upon the new crop, which would grow abundantly. At the end of the year it would be burned and the ashes ploughed back into the fields ready to enrich the next sowing.

It has been suggested that the corn dollies are part of an older tradition, dating back to ancient times. When early people settled down, giving up their nomadic hunter-gatherer existence and first began to farm, they believed that the gods needed to be petitioned in order for their crops to thrive. Sacrifices and ceremonies would take place so that the gods would protect the crops and the communities that consumed them. These ceremonies and practices occurred all round the world. Ceres, the corn goddess of ancient Rome, and Demeter, the Greek goddess of the harvest, or Isis, the fertility goddess of ancient Egypt, have been linked to similar cyclic rituals of renewal and harvest. Corn effigies had a variety of names such as Clyack, Corn Maiden, Harvest Maid, Kern Baby, Churn, Hag and Mare.

The term Corn Dolly is a modern one, first used in the twentieth century. Traditionally, each county in England has its own Corn Dolly design. There are, for example, the Stafford Knot, the Cambridge Umbrella, and the Suffolk Horseshoe. Many of these Dollies do not look like people but are knot designs such as spirals and horseshoes. There is also a tradition in England of 'Countrymen's Favours' – woven hearts and circles tied to represent eternity.

The Wicker Man film, directed by Robin Hardy and released in 1973, featured a huge wicker edifice used for a ritualistic sacrifice. The film was shot in and around Plockton, Newton Stewart, Kirkcudbright and at Culzean Castle in Ayrshire, now owned by The National Trust. The Wicker Man itself, burned at the end of the film, was constructed at Burrowhead in Scotland, now the site of a caravan park. The stumps from the burned effigy remained at the site for three decades but were eventually cut down and stolen in 2006. The idea of ritualised sacrifice by burning inside an effigy was suggested by ancient Romans Julius Caesar and Strabo, who claimed that the druids of Gaul burned sacrifices in great wicker effigies. He wrote that the Celts *'possess woven wicker figures of vast size that they fill with living people; which, being set on fire, the people are engulfed in flames and killed'. (Commentarii de Bello Gallico*, I.6. c.16)

This idea has been largely discredited by modern day scholars. However, effigies have been burned in ceremonies around the world. In parts of northern Portugal in the present day, gigantic human effigies called *Entrudo* are burned as part of the centuries-old Caretos Festival that announces spring. The festival reaches a crescendo when the figure is burned as people run around it. Fortunately, no human sacrifices are required...

Wicker men are also burned during the commemorative Wicker Man music festival held in Kirkcudbrightshire, Scotland (where much of the 1973 film was shot on location). On the Saturday night, at midnight, the iconic 30ft wicker man, build by local artisans Trevor Leat and Alex Rigg, is burned. A wicker man is also burned at the eponymous Burning Man Festival in the Black Rock Desert, Nevada. This arts event was first held in 1986 in San Francisco by Larry Harvey and Jerry James, who built the first woven giant.

Chapter 10

Woven boats

In 1974 an excavation at Barns Farm in Dalgety, Fife, unearthed a Bronze Age burial site containing what were eventually identified as coracles which had been used as coffins. These lightweight traditional boats were made from split wood and woven withies made into a frame, covered in skin such as horse or ox hide for waterproofing. They were usually built upside down, with hazel rods being driven into the ground on a circle. When a cage-type frame had been built, willow withies were woven between the rods along the ground, creating a rim. The hazel rods were then bent over to create a basket-like dome. The hide (cow, horse or even seal) covering was lashed to the boat frame and waterproofed with fat such as tallow or even butter.

They were used for fishing in the rivers and shallow bays around the coast of Wales, in the West Country, in Scotland (particularly along the River Spey) and in Ireland. *Coracle* is the anglicized version of the welsh *cwrwgl*. In Irish and Scottish Gaelic the boats were called *currach* or *curragh*. They were woven from wicker and waterproofed with leather hides. The frame, in Gaelic, was called a *crannghail*.

In 1527 Hector Boece wrote a history of Scotland and chronicled the use of these vessels in the Highlands:

> *How be it, the Highlanders have both the writings and language they had before, more ingenious than any other people. How may there be any greater ingenuity than to make any boat of any bull-hide,*

bound with nothing but wands? This boat is called a curragh, *and with it they fish salmon ... and when they have done their fishing they bear it to another place on their back as they please.*

Coracles look like half a walnut and have no keel. They have a flat bottom, which spreads the load inside the boat and means the boat can manoeuvre in very shallow water – as little as a few inches. This makes it an excellent vessel for fishing in rivers. When skilfully moved across the surface of the waters with a traditional broad paddle, they barely disturb the surface. This makes them wonderful for fishermen as the fish barely see them coming!

Traditional construction varied a little from area to area. On the tidal *River Tywi* or *Afon Tywi,* the traditional Carmarthen coracle was rounded and deep. It was made from sawn, split ash and used copper nails. On the *River Teifi* or *Afon Teifi* the coracle was flatter bottomed and less rounded, as it was made to traverse the shallow rapids common on the river. It was made from willow laths to create the body frame of the boat and woven hazel for the weave. The interweaving made it strong and negated the need for nails. Coracles were light and intended to be carried on the back of the fisherman. There is even a Welsh saying: *Llwyth dyn ei gorwgl* – the load of a man is his coracle.

Coracles were used to net and gather fish and eels from traps in rivers, and to gather the catch from lobster pots along the coast. The traps were, of course, baskets just like the boats. They were also used to transport passengers and goods between islands.

Woven boats of different types were made around the world. In Tibet people sailed in the *Ku-Dru or Kowa*, woven from wood and covered in Yak skin. In the Middle East, the *quffah* (also known as *kuphar, kufa, kuffah* or *kuphar*) looks like a basket made for carrying fruits or vegetables – and, indeed that is where the origin of the word comes from.

A *quffa* is a basket woven from reeds and leaves and a *quppu* is a basket. Some were made from a woven framework covered in skins, and others were woven from bundles of reeds and sewn together like a basket before being waterproofed with a thick coat of bitumen. *Quffas* are boats from antiquity; it has even been suggested that the biblical Ark was in fact a large quffa, as was the basket in which Moses was said to be set adrift on the Nile. They were mentioned by the Ancient Greek historian Herodotus who described them when he visited Babylon in around 450BC.

But that which surprises me most in the land, after the city itself, I will now proceed to mention. The boats which come down the river to Babylon are circular and made of skins. The frames, which are of willow, are cut in the country of the Armenians above Assyria, and on these, which serve for hulls, a covering of skins is stretched outside, and thus the boats are made, without either stem or stern, quite round like a shield. They are then entirely filled with straw, and their cargo is put on board, after which they are suffered to float down the stream. Their chief freight is wine, stored in casks made of the wood of the palm tree. They are managed by two men who stand upright in them, each plying an oar, one pulling and the other pushing. The boats are of various sizes, some larger, some smaller; the biggest reach as high as five thousand talents burthen. Each vessel has a live ass on board; those of larger size have more than one. When they reach Babylon, the cargo is landed and offered for sale; after which the men break up their boats, sell the straw and the frames, and loading their asses with the skins, set off on their way back to Armenia. The current is too strong to allow a boat to return upstream, for which reason they make their boats of skins rather than wood. On their return to Armenia they build fresh boats for the next voyage. (Herodotus)

These boats were still being used in 1938 when James Hornell, the British ethnographer wrote his book *The coracles of the Tigris and Euphrates*.

> *...the craft likened in form to the Tibetan food-bowl—perfectly circular in plan, nearly flat bottomed, and with convexly curved sides that tumble-home to join the stout cylindrical gunwale bounding the mouth, which is several inches less in diameter than the width at mid height. In construction a quffa is just a huge lidless basket, strengthened within by innumerable ribs radiating from around the centre of the floor. The type of basketry employed is of that widely distributed kind termed coiled basketry.*

Quffas were still being used in Iraq until the 1970s as water taxis, for transporting goods and as fishing boats.

In America, First People made similar crafts called Bull Boats – a framework made from willow woven in a bowl shape and then covered in buffalo hides. The hair was left on the hides to keep water out and to help to prevent the craft from spinning as it moved along on the surface of the water. The tails were often left on the hides and were used to tie the boats together in a kind of convoy. When fur traders from the Hudson's Bay Company first came to trade with the Mandan tribe in the 1790s, they noticed the boats. By the early 1800s, fur traders were building boats using the traditional methods, but longer to transport huge quantities of furs down the river to trading posts.

The Lewis and Clark Expedition (1804-1806), commissioned by President Thomas Jefferson, was the first expedition of settled Americans across the (to white settlers) uncharted west. It was made up of US Army volunteers under the command of Captain Merriwether Lewis and Lieutenant William Clark. Its purpose was to chart the territory; to find a route across it and to establish an American presence before claims were made by the British or other European powers. The expedition studied the flora and fauna of the country as well as the geography. It was also expected to establish trade agreements with local tribes. The expedition described the Bull Boats in this way:

Two sticks of 1¼ inch diameter are tied together so as to form a round hoop of the size you wish the canoe to be, or as large as the skin will cover. Two of those hoops are made, one for the top or brim, and the other for the bottom. Then sticks of the same diameter are crossed at right angles and fastened with a thong to each hoop, and also where each stick crosses the other. Then the skin, when green [fresh, that is, not tanned] *is drawn tight over the frame and fastened with thongs to the brim, or outer hoop, so as to form a perfect basin.*

Similar boats were woven in Vietnam, made from woven bamboo which was waterproofed with a mixture of coconut oil mixed with resin. Inuit women made woven boats called *umiak* ('open boat') which were waterproofed with sealskin.

It is incredible to think that humble plant fibre can help to feed communities and move them from place to place by being used to make boats that can sail down rivers, across lakes and even out on the ocean.

Chapter 11

Artisan Interviews

The best way to find out about the modern artisans working in basketry today, is to ask them about their experiences, inspirations and artistic practices. With the advent of the internet, it is easier than ever to find a window into the creative world of these artisans and to find out more.

These artists and crafters earn a living with their craft. They have taken the leap into self-employment and sustain themselves and their families with their skill and artistry. I asked the artists a series of questions, and encouraged them to describe their motivations, inspirations and goals for the future. They have taken traditional techniques and allowed them to evolve as they have explored their own ways of working.

You can find out more about each artist by following the links provided for their websites and social media. You can also buy their products directly, or even commission pieces yourself, and help to support the hand-made industry directly at source! Some of these artisans also offer courses to teach you how to create your own basketry items.

John Cowan Baskets
What first attracted you to your craft?
I was always good with working with my hands. I decided I wanted to work in traditional crafts, so I set about looking for and signing up to

courses in these. I attended dry-stone walling, which was great, but I simply couldn't lift the big stones I would want to use to make a really good strong wall. So that was out. I tried a bit of leatherwork, but I am a veggie (pescatarian anyway) so that didn't sit right with me. I tried roof slating and again loved working with stone but the uncomfortable working position at height was the drawback. The thing I really did pursue for over a year was wooden clinker boat building. I built a boat (which I used on the Forth-Clyde canal for a number of years after) and was on my way with my second. To learn any craft we have to practise, practise, practise. Therefore, if I had continued my training in this I would have absolutely bankrupted myself buying all the high-quality timber, woodworking tools and other materials so this unfortunately realistically couldn't continue. (Boat building is a very noisy thing too and my neighbours would have lost patience with me after much more of it, I expect.)

During all this, I had been attending one-day willow weaving workshops, 1-to-1 and found myself continuing to enjoy this and not give in to the considerable challenges, so I decided to become a bit more serious about this. Basket making requires very little tools (usually less than what the beginner goes out and buys when they start out in the craft!) and it is relatively cheap to make the many baskets needed to begin to develop competency in the craft. I was seriously ill for a year, unable to work at the day job, and was recovering for about a year after that. During this time I made baskets and I got the benefit of the rhythmic therapy and developed my skills considerably. After recovery, I found I had the skills to make baskets people would buy and come back and buy again. I decided I owed it to myself and must try to make a go of this and do basket making professionally. It was tough financially at first. I had to sacrifice a lot. But it has been worth it.

Can you describe your journey into your craft? How did you get started? For example, do you have particular training or qualifications, or are you self-taught?

Following from the above, I decided on the style of baskets I like best, baskets of the British basketmaking tradition, and I sought tuition from makers who were, quite simply, doing what I wanted to be doing. (Initially Geoff Forrest, Lise Bech then Vigilijus Bauzys and Colin Manthorpe.) I think what was essential here was to be prepared to travel and seek out the best people for me and be prepared to pay for their time to enable them to give me the quality one-to-one tuition needed to train to be a professional basket maker. The training for me looked like one, two or three days back-to-back training with my teachers in their workshops. Then going away and practising what they showed me over several months. Then taking examples of my work back to them for criticism and getting more tuition and repeating this process.

I'll mention, during this time I attended small craft fairs and sold my baskets (mostly at a price where they were likely to sell, I have to say) seeing the public reaction was useful, I learned what sort of baskets were popular and what styles were appreciated. This proved useful when building my business and also provided me with a direction to pursue in my training. A sale is a huge compliment and I didn't have the burden of all my practice baskets building up, and this gave me the motivation to make more to take to a sale. I think the main training to enable me to do the job fully lasted about five years.

Do you have any inspirations or influences? This could include particular artisans, periods in history etc.

I like the professional British basket making tradition, a method probably refined I guess for the market during the period of the Industrial Revolution up until the start of the use of plastic containers.

This, I would say, is characterised by baskets made with chunky materials, often with beautiful large borders. The British craftsmen cleverly came up with a style of beautiful strong baskets but with the potential to be produced relatively quickly, without compromising on quality and durability. Most of these craftspeople were anonymous and yet it is a wonderful legacy they have left for us. I looked around and didn't see all that many makers working in this style today, there seems to be more doing fine intricate work, often spending several days making one basket, than there is working in the traditional quality utilitarian way. That slow-process way of working wouldn't be my sort of thing and I imagine it would be difficult forming a business from it. Most of those folk do a lot of teaching I've noticed. I decided I could give most by working in the traditional style, especially since some of the almost iconic British designs were at risk of dying out.

What do you enjoy most about working with the materials that you choose to work with?
I enjoy when I am able to source without very much difficulty the ever-scarcening basketmaking willows that I need to secure to fulfill orders from my customers. It takes just as much skill to grow quality basketmaking willows as it does to weave baskets and good growers these days are a rare and precious thing.

Please describe the tools of your craft, and how you use them.
Very few tools are needed to make baskets; a knife and secateurs are the basics. I'm sure you will discuss the tools elsewhere in the book but the two most important things for a beginner, I would say, are not to go mad buying tons of tools that are available. When I started, besides the above, I used an old big spanner to knock down the weave, which was absolutely fine instead of the rapping iron, and I ground a rounded bit of scrap

metal rod into a spike for my bodkin. These served me well at no cost. The second thing is the huge importance of working on the plank. It takes hands, arms, legs, feet (chin, teeth... and so on!) to control the work and make a good basket. I think it would be mostly a waste of time to try to make a good basket sitting at tables and chairs. Therefore, we need a large raised plank to sit on, so we can sweep all the snipped ends off this and they fall down and don't get in the way and irritate, and the smaller plank sits on top of this to make the baskets on. This sits between the knees when the basket is upset and the sides are being woven so the maker can get at it with all limbs.

Describe your business. What items do you make? Do you sell items – if so, what? Do you teach courses? Describe the thing you have made that has made you most proud.

I make a lot of custom-made baskets to customer specifications, such as rectangular baskets to fit onto shelving for storage in the kitchen etc. Besides these, the totally unexpected requests are frequently things I never thought I'd make yet have been commissioned from me like huge baskets which two actors can sit inside with the lid shut. I made a large eye-catching basket from which free condoms would be offered to athletes in the athletes' village at a somewhat important international sporting event and baskets to hold bombs for a film production. I'm no longer surprised by requests by email.

I also make a standard range of traditional basket designs which I sell online which I make over and over again. Rather than dull repetition, these baskets are the ones I look forward to making and enjoy making the most. I think of all the anonymous hands who would have known these styles and made these regularly throughout their careers. Making these are what I am most proud of. Most of all, amongst these, the quarter *cran* herring basket is my favourite and it took me many years of very hard work to learn to make that difficult basket. Doing this allowed me to be one of the few people who can really appreciate the lives and skills of the basket makers who went to work and made six, eight or even ten of this style every day for a whole season and would only be paid if their work was absolutely perfect. And, of course, it was. Wonderful people and I don't know how they did it and I find their stoical lives inspirational.

Please describe a typical day.
The typical day starts with emails. Then, wrapping baskets for posting if I have orders to fulfil that day. Working in the workshop 10 'til 6 is usual then more emails in the evening. You have to work really hard, I'm afraid, to earn a secure regular income as a basket maker and I often work six days in the week.

What traditional 'heritage' methods do you use in your craft?
In the traditional baskets I make, it is important to make the pattern just as it has always been made without making changes. The specifications are recorded and handed down to us. The work would seem to have more value to me if care is taken with this.

How have you adapted heritage or historic methods for the modern day?
The most important thing for my basket making business is the internet. Selling online directly to customers from my website is the biggest source of income. I do a little wholesale work and attend a few shows selling and demonstrating, but my main income comes from online sales. Thank goodness I don't have to rely on selling to shops etc like the old makers had to deal with. This way of working can be lonely, however, but there is a strong community of basket makers who keep in touch through Instagram and such and this has been helpful and I've benefited from this exchange.

What advice would you give someone starting out in your field?

Do your research and see what's going on and try to find someone doing as close as possible to what you want to be doing then try and get as much training from them as you can. Be prepared to travel and pay for their time. Basket making is difficult and requires many late nights working into the small hours in freezing sheds, so you need to be sure it is what you want to do. Check this out by practice of what you've learned in your own time and if you find yourself still interested then the craft might be for you. Basket making can be frustrating and unforgiving. Remember, if you have encountered a difficulty, as the craft is thousands of years old, someone else probably has had the same trouble in the past! There will be a solution to the problem and the basket maker community is generally friendly, so ask for some suggestions in one of the many online social media willow weaving groups.

Website: www.johncowanbaskets.co.uk

Anna Turnbull – Biteabout Arts

What first attracted you to your craft?

The rhythm of weaving willow, its fluidity so hypnotic, so natural, so innate.

Can you describe your journey into your craft? How did you get started? For example, do you have particular training or qualifications, or are you self-taught?

I did a Fine Art Degree initially and have always enjoyed creating. Eight years ago, having made baskets at school and wanting to revisit this experience, my mother saw a course advertised and together we participated. I was hooked.

Do you have any inspirations or influences? This could include particular artisans, periods in history etc.
Jo Hoggan, Lise Beck, Lizzie Farey and Jenny Crisp are all makers whose work I admire. Nature's diverse forms, colours, influence my creations.

What do you enjoy most about working with the materials that you choose to work with?
With willow, the fluidity of the soaked rods, their ability to create three-dimensional objects, their sustainability, the fact I can grow them.

Please describe the tools of your craft, and how you use them.
For willow – a knife for scalloming, a bodkin for prizing open spaces in the work, secateurs for trimming rods, rapping iron for beating and compacting the work, a fid for threading rods through sculptures

Describe your business. What items do you make? Do you sell items – if so, what? Do you teach courses? Describe the thing you have made that has made you most proud.
I make willow baskets, traditional and contemporary, willow sculptures. I also make felt items and combine felt work with my willow work. I sell my work at events, exhibitions and encourage commissions. I teach workshops in basketry, willow sculpture and felt making.

I am proud of my willow animals, especially those with movement, the squirrel that looks as if it has been startled as it scurries away.

Please describe a typical day.
There are many variations on a typical day, as it could be a teaching day, a harvesting day, a making day, a selling or publicising day, an admin day. On a making day, the rods would have been soaked for up to a week,

then taken out of the tank the previous day and wrapped in old blanket to mellow somewhere cool overnight.

A basket base would be started with a small hoop, rods inserted to create both base sticks and uprights. After a few rounds of pairing to space the uprights and grow the base, the uprights would be eased into shape. The weaving of the sides with French Rand would begin. The shape would be constantly assessed, changed, balanced and openings for felt could be created, the felt shapes cut from a piece made the previous day.

What traditional 'heritage' methods do you use in your craft?
Weaving willow rods using traditional weaves to create traditional style baskets.

How have you adapted heritage or historic methods for the modern day?
I experiment with new forms and combine materials.

What advice would you give someone starting out in your field?
Practise, learn from the experts, join an organisation such as the Basketry Association.

About me:
I was born on 10 June 1966 in Newcastle and after graduating in 1988 with BA Hons in Fine Art from Camberwell School of Arts, I returned home to Northumberland to work as a photographic artist and silversmith. In 1994 I trained to teach and then worked in schools whilst continuing on my own creative journey.

I started experimenting with the many processes in the making of felt in 2005. I fell in love with its versatility, being able 'to paint' with a varied palette of dyed wools, create something delicate and ephemeral using fine wools and silks, or use more sculptural techniques to form vessels. In 2010 I was introduced to the many varieties of coloured willows grown locally for basketry and the traditional techniques used to work with them. It excited me and I started using these to create vessels and sculptures.

I set up Biteabout Arts in 2011 to work as a self-employed fibre artist using these media to create artworks. Enjoying teaching, I also run workshops and deliver courses at various venues including my studio.

My work is inspired by the rural landscape in which I live and work. I reference the wildlife, the organic forms, the rich colours and textures of nature. I grow a variety of willows, using this and other locally grown materials in my work.

Website: www.biteabout.co.uk

Eddie Glew Baskets – Blithfield Willowcrafts

What first attracted you to your craft?

I fell into the craft really and I have my father to thank, he was a first class basketmaker himself. I was 20 years old and in between jobs having been laid off as a trainee electrician. It wasn't something I searched for, basketmaking found me.

Can you describe your journey into your craft? How did you get started? For example, do you have particular training or qualifications, or are you self-taught?

I've had two main teachers in my life so far and lots of help from other makers like Adrian Charlton and Francois Desplanches. Firstly, my father, who I worked with for two years, he tried to teach me everything he could and in such a way as to peak my interest. Dad's tuition and guidance sparked my love for the craft and its limitless possibilities.

My second mentor, whom I also trained with for two years, is Sally Goymer. I have her to thank for where I am today. She feeds my need for knowledge, new techniques, encourages, shows me that hard work pays off. She showed me that the small things make a huge difference, being meticulous with your material selection for example and making precise work. These are the things that will make your work pop and stand out, although not obviously to the untrained eye.

Both my mentors were honest enough as well to tell me when my work wasn't up to standard, which taught me to be self-critical, which ultimately is the only way to keep improving. Dad's favourite saying was 'that will look great in the garden, son'. Overall I've been very fortunate and had mentorship from one maker or another throughout my nine years of making. I've never been afraid to ask for help which I think is a good thing.

Do you have any inspirations or influences? This could include particular artisans, periods in history etc.
My main influences in the craft for the quality of their work as well as what they've passed on to me are Sally Goymer, François Desplanches and Adrian Charlton. The main influence on my life and craft is my father, the way he led his life, simple but meaningful, with self-discipline, living in the present, nothing wasted, words or time, is a mantra I try to live up to but fail every day!

What do you enjoy most about working with the materials that you choose to work with?
Willow is so diverse, from the different varieties and colours to the way it grows and its different thicknesses. Willow's versatility allows us as makers to create lots of different things and experiment as the material is so forgiving. My favourite species is *purpurea*, the rods are generally

slender and when soaked correctly are beautiful to work. The fact that a bunch of tampered sticks can be transformed into something beautiful and useful for decades to come is special.

Please describe the tools of your craft, and how you use them.
The beauty of our craft is that a basket can be made with just a knife. The more precise you want your work to be, the more tools you'll use. The basic tools are: a bodkin (a pointed tool), rapping iron (for bashing down and tightening work) and snips. Other essential tools are a tape measure, curved bodkin, string, tallow, knife. Other tools for square work and 'made to measure work' are a hammer, nails, jigs and moulds.

Describe your business. What items do you make? Do you sell items – if so, what? Do you teach courses? Describe the thing you have made that has made you most proud.
My business – Blithfield Willowcrafts – is all things willow. Running a craft business is great fun and being diverse in what you do is key to constantly bringing the money in. My passion is basket making and my skill is in this, but I also make willow sculpture, willow fencing, living willow, attend shows and festivals and of course teaching. I run my own workshops as well as teach the City and Guilds Basketry at Westhope Craft College in Shropshire.

Please describe a typical day.
I base my day always around food! In truth no day is the same. I may be teaching abroad one week, then in a restaurant installing some woven light fittings the next, to sitting in the workshop making basket commissions the week after. Our work is portable, so I often work in evenings and being your own boss allows you to be flexible with your time.

What traditional 'heritage' methods do you use in your craft?
I'm a traditional basket maker so all I make technique-wise has been passed down from generation to generation. Hand on heart I can say all I make is copied and are repeated patterns and weaves; I'm proud of this fact and this is the main reason I love what I do. I'm a tiny link in a chain that goes back thousands of years and I can't wait to pass on what I know later in my career. I'm also all for moving the craft forward, being innovative and encourage all makers to do this.

How have you adapted heritage or historic methods for the modern day?
Traditional basket making techniques in my opinion give you the best foundation for using the material 'willow'. With these I've woven lamp shades, wall and ceiling pieces for restaurants, done theming for an Alton Towers ride, made baskets for royalty and woven a living willow maze at Warwick Castle. All of these made easier from my basket making skill set.

What advice would you give someone starting out in your field?
You need a solid base of techniques. They're like tools in your tool box, the more you have, the easier it is to complete any job. Try and do something productive that is willow-related every day. You have to be passionate about the craft to make it your living, but passion alone isn't enough, like most things there's no substitute for working hard, which has been instilled in me by all my mentors. Be prepared to work seven days a week, do jobs you don't like and never hesitate to seek more knowledge. It's a privilege having this job and never take it for granted...lastly never undersell yourself, you're worth what people will pay.
Website: www.blithfieldwillowcrafts.co.uk

Colette Basketry

What first attracted you to your craft?

I have an Art and Design background having completed A Levels in Textiles and Sculpture. I then went on to do an Art Foundation year at the Surrey Institute of Art and Design. Following that I completed a BA Hons degree in Visual Communication in 1999 also in Surrey.

My love of basketry first got ignited a few years ago when I went on a willow basketry course with my friend and continuing mentor Judy Hartley; the course took place in her barn/workshop at her home in Usk. I remember walking in and falling in love with the sweet smell of all the willow in there and being in awe of all her baskets that were hanging around her home. I think I was pretty much hooked straight away. I loved the grounding earthiness of working with this natural material, the smell, the physical nature of it, how when you worked time slipped by and you had to be totally focused in the moment.

Can you describe your journey into your craft? How did you get started? For example, do you have particular training or qualifications, or are you self-taught?

Last year I completed a City and Guilds in Basketry at Westhope Craft College, my tutor was Eddie Glew of Blithfield Willow Crafts and I obtained a Distinction. The bulk of the teaching during the course was in willow basketry with a bit of rush work, but we were encouraged to explore other basketry materials too as this was an integral part of the course criteria. I think all the reading and researching about other basket makers and fibre artists I carried out as part of my coursework was when the world of basketry possibilities really opened up for me and my interest in fibre basketry began.

Although I have obviously been taught in willow basketry and had tuition on a small amount of twining techniques, I am self-taught in coil basketry which is the type of basketry I mainly create now. I am also self-taught with the help of a few books and snippets of advice from other basket makers and artists on Instagram – the knowledge I now have about harvesting, processing and using local garden and wild plants to use in basketry.

Do you have any inspirations or influences? This could include particular artisans, periods in history etc.

I am very influenced by all the amazing fibre basket makers and fibre artists all over the world I connect with via Instagram, especially those in Australia. I also own a copy of the book which is often known as the 'Fibre Basketry Bible' among fellow fibre artists (especially Australian ones). It is called *Fibre Basketry, Homegrown and Handmade* by The Fibre Basket Weavers of South Australia Inc, edited by Helen Richardson. As well as in-depth information on many coil basketry techniques, it has amazing information on how to process and use numerous species of plants, including Australian ones and many that grow here. This book has certainly become my bible!

Closer to home I love the work of Tim Johnson, who is based in Spain but regularly travels and teaches around the world including in the UK. I was delighted to be able to attend Tim's course in Looping, Netting and Knotting in July 2018 at West Dean College in Sussex.

What do you enjoy most about working with the materials that you choose to work with?

I love the process of finding, gathering and drying plant parts! I love the experimentation, the slightly unknown outcome, seeing a plant and wondering how it would work, look, how strong it would be once it is dried and then re-soaked. This process takes ages and I am never going to be churning out baskets at a great speed, but this is what I love; the total process from start to finish with all the learning along the way. As I work, I love the smell of damp plant fibre and the feel of it. Also, the soothing repetitive rhythms and the way my hands gain their muscle memories.

Please describe the tools of your craft, and how you use them.
I use very few tools in fibre basketry, even fewer than with willow basketry. I have a collection of needles, mainly ones with a very large eye that is big enough to fit fibre of waxed linen thread. I have a mixture of blunt-ended or sharp Chenille ones depending which technique I am using. I use a fine, very sharp, pair of scissors for trimming fibre. I couldn't manage without my water spray, which I use to dampen my fibres down when they have dried out as I am working with them. I sometimes use a sharp knife to cut strips of things like bark or roots. My most recent tool which I am very pleased with, is an old football lacer. It is similar to a huge blunt needle which is great for getting between layers of fibre in a basket without damaging them and pulling fibres through small gaps. I soak fibres mainly in the bath and keep them damp for working by wrapping them up in a towel or blanket.

Describe your business. What items do you make? Do you sell items – if so, what? Do you teach courses? Describe the thing you have made that has made you most proud.
I am still in the process of setting up my business and building my website. I use Instagram and Facebook to promote myself and link up with other makers across the world. I sell my baskets at The Court Cupboard Craft Gallery and through social media. I am slowly increasing my teaching, focusing mainly on coil basketry techniques both at the Gallery and back

at Westhope Craft College. I returned to teach Coil Basketry on the two City and Guilds Basketry courses that are running there this year and will be teaching on another City and Guilds Basketry course taught by Clare Revera in South Wales later on in the year. I have a few course ideas in the pipeline, including short ones in cordage and string-making from different plant fibres.

I think the two pieces that I am currently most proud of are two large coil technique wall hangings. One is made of different types of iris leaves and stitched with waxed linen thread and the other is made of a mixture of leaves and roots and linen thread. Both I made when I felt I had finally totally got to grips with a particular technique and fibre.

Please describe a typical day.
I don't really have a typical day! I know it's a bit of a cliché to say every day is different, but it is, often because I am juggling children, animals and other work commitments. Some days the nearest I get to a full day's work is between morning school drop off and afternoon school pick up. Most evenings I am weaving things after the children are in bed. I have days when I spend hours gathering and then laying out plant materials to dry. These can be anything from dandelion flower stems and nettles, roots to day lily leaves and everything in between. Then comes loads of turning and tying up in bundles once things are dry enough. Then re-tying in bundles when it has dried some more and shrunk. My house looks like a barn with bits of plant fibre absolutely everywhere. I also usually have at least three baskets or wall hangings on the go which I dip in and out of, I prefer to work like this instead of just doing one thing from start to finish. It allows me to pause with a project and often resolve a problem before coming back to it. I am part of a co-operative gallery, the Court Cupboard Craft Gallery which is part of the Black Mountain Craft Circle. I open up and run the gallery there twice a month. Sometimes I also teach there.

What traditional 'heritage' methods do you use in your craft?
Coil basketry is a method where relatively short lengths of fibre can be used to build up a continuous core, these are then securely 'stitched' with more fibre or thread. These baskets were mainly produced in hot countries where the plant fibres are more plentiful; that said, the bee skep is an example of a coiled technique that is a UK tradition that continues to this day.

Producing cordage has been a vital part of people's lives for thousands of years; people need cordage to aid carriage, build shelter, catch food etc. I use traditional cordage-making techniques; many of the fibres that I use would have been used by my ancestors going back many centuries.

How have you adapted heritage or historic methods for the modern day?
People no longer need to make functional baskets or cordage; I create these for the joy and pleasure of working with the materials, the aesthetically pleasing outcome and hoping to sustain traditional techniques in the modern era. The techniques are essentially unchanged; the basics are the same, but the functional use of the final product is no longer the only option, I can make art pieces as well as cordage and baskets. I have also adapted the techniques slightly to be able to use sea plastic, marine rubbish that I have collected on the shores of South Wales; essentially, coil basketry techniques can be utilised with almost any fibrous material. The sea plastic link is relevant in that historically, plant fibre cordage would have been used to make the nets. Any missing 'ghost nets' would soon have been degraded by the ocean, unlike the modern-day plastic fibres.

What advice would you give someone starting out in your field?
I would advise that people speak to existing basket makers who, by and large, are willing to share their knowledge. The basketry world is relatively small and friendly and people want to pass on their skills to others, ensuring that traditional techniques are not lost.

Sculptural hanging art baskets created by Mae Adams.

Above left: Sumptuously textural basket created by artist Mae Adams.

Above right: This beautiful coiled mat made with wrapped garlic fibre is by artist Mae Adams.

Colette Davies from Colette Basketry loves the process of collecting and drying plants and the subtle shading of this piece is a great example of her art.

Above left: A simple cord but a thing of beauty from Colette Basketry.

Above right: This perfect pot was created by Colette Basketry.

Colette Davies has great skill in showing the natural beauty of the materials she selects for her art.

This bold statement piece from Colette Basketry revels in the hues of a summer moorland.

Above left: An intricately woven piece from Colette Basketry.

Above right: A mesmerising pattern from Colette Basketry.

Delicate meadow hues in this lovely piece woven by Colette Davies.

Bright, beautiful ropes used to great effect by Colette Davies.

Blue Moon is a stunning sculpture by Pamela Zimmermann.

Catching the Moon is a gorgeous sculpture by Pamela Zimmermann.

Above left: This beautiful willow fox is from Anna Turnbull at Biteabout Arts.

Above right: These lovely autumnal vessels from Anna Turnbull use a flash of felt for colour.

These watchful willow deer were woven by Eddie Glew at Blithfield Willowcrafts.

The contrasting colours and clean design of these baskets from Eddie Glew Basketry are a joy to behold.

This willow foal by Anna Turnbull looks ready to take flight across the fields.

About me:

I live in Monmouthshire in the beautiful Wye Valley with my husband, children, lurchers and chickens. As well as basketry I like to walk in the woods, spend time with family and potter in the garden.

Website: http://**colettedavies.co.uk**

I'm @colettebasketry on various platforms, here are the links:

Instagram: https://www.instagram.com/colettebasketry

Facebook: https://www.facebook.com/colettebasketry

Twitter: https://twitter.com/colettebasketry

Pamela Zimmerman

What first attracted you to your craft?

I have always wanted to make things. Working as a Park Ranger with the National Park Service brought me to the US desert southwest, and there I was exposed to many Native American crafts. The basketry spoke most to me, even though I could afford little of it. Pottery, rugs and carved wood, and even jewellery were all more accessible – less expensive – than the baskets. Baskets are fragile and made of materials that deteriorate and are not made by many craftsmen. If you go to Santa Fe right now, on the square, where Native people sit with their hand crafts, you will not find a basket maker among them. Because it is too time consuming and expensive. But those were the things that spoke to me most, and what I wanted to do, and so I learned to make them.

Can you describe your journey into your craft? How did you get started? For example, do you have particular training or qualifications, or are you self-taught?

I left the Park Service, and became a full-time mother to two very active and challenging boys. Someone gave me a gift certificate from a bookstore, and I picked a how-to coiling book, Judy *Mallow's Pine Needle Basketry:*

From Forest Floor to Finished Project. The title said exactly what I wanted to do. It was something I could literally do in the yard, picking up pine needles as I went, so I could do it while watching the boys play.

I could not find anyone else making pine needle baskets near me, so I started a website to gather other coilers together, and this brought me into the forefront of the basketry community online. From there, I figured out what worked for me (not like it was in the book!) and spent years convincing myself it was okay to deviate from the techniques I saw in the book…and convincing other people they could deviate, too!

After learning in isolation for a few years, I attended a basketry convention, where I took my first actual basket class. I have some classes over the years, to learn different techniques, or use materials that I do not normally have access to (like willow or ash.) Then I explore the application of those techniques by myself, trying to adapt what I saw in a video online, or in a book, to use what I already have, and make… something. I have a studio now, though, no more coiling in the yard, with pine needles picked up as I go. I have branched out into many other techniques, but I still coil. I have been doing it now for twenty years.

Do you have any inspirations or influences? This could include particular artisans, periods in history etc.

My original inspiration was aboriginal basketry, beginning with that of the Hopi, Pima and Navajo. But all tribal-style craft intrigues me and influences me. My life, family, children also inspire me. Many of the pieces that people tell me are the most compelling were inspired by my life and its challenges, like my 'Catching the Moon' series. I generally do not try to work on a focused theme but find there are ones that seem to repeat in my work, and they return to my relationship with my children and my role as a mother. Birth, rebirth, cocooning, transition, transformation, metamorphosis, emergence, change, and perspectives on these processes often are apparent in my work.

What do you enjoy most about working with the materials that you choose to work with?

I like best to use what I have, if I can, to make things…I really try to resist going to the store to buy something. I like best to collect material, whether it be something that is growing, or from the recycle bin. I have to say I am quite prejudiced toward something that someone else might consider trash. I like to be able to say what is recycled in my work, and sometimes I save things for years before I use them. I like it when it is free and when nobody else really wants it. Where I live, pine needles are called 'pine straw' and considered mulch.

Please describe the tools of your craft, and how you use them.

Coiling is my most often used method. I use various large-eyed needles of many sizes, sharp and blunted, for coiling. I also use scissors, pliers, knives, awls, flat-shaped packers (sort of like screwdrivers,) that sort of thing. I did invent my 'Needle Grabbers' which are made of rubber, and worn on the ends of the fingers, for pulling a needle through a basket. They are very useful. I collect things like hammers and other tools. I can't describe the myriad ways I use them and admit that I just like tools…sometimes I pick up one just to have it, because I am sure I will need it one day.

Describe your business. What items do you make? Do you sell items – if so, what? Do you teach courses? Describe the thing you have made that has made you most proud.

When I first began weaving, I worked exclusively as a studio artist, doing fine art shows and showing in galleries. I did that for over ten years, exploring many basketry techniques. I developed my own techniques for horsehair coiling, something there are no books explaining, and which is generally left to a few select native weavers.

Then, while pushing myself to prepare for a gallery exhibition, I began to have trouble with my hands and shoulders, from repetitive motion. I had to change the way I did things, including my expectations. I could no longer spend eight to ten hours in the studio, and plan elaborate art pieces. I could barely weave for an hour a day, and that only if I iced my body, did a bunch of exercises, had medical care.

So I switched to mainly teaching basketry and selling my work on Etsy.com. I started out only selling my finished artwork on Etsy, but soon branched out into basketry supplies, by request of my students. Later, I added a separate shop for woven wearables (jewellery). I had been incorporating pottery into my fine art work for years, but began making stoneware basket starts for students, and eventually branched out into functional pottery, as well. About the past 5 years, I have another side business, where I make ornaments from post-consumer aluminum beverage cans…but that is pretty much only from about October through a week before Christmas. But, in spite of all the other things I do, I still consider myself, first and foremost, a basket maker.

Now that I must limit my weaving hours, to preserve my hands and shoulders, I tend to make very small pieces. Most of my weaving is related to teaching, now. I do also make natural baskets, made of gathered materials that are chemical and pesticide free, and sell them on Etsy as 'green' baskets for weddings – flower girl baskets.

I like my Catching the Moon series, if I had to pick my favorite work, it might be my 'Catching the Pale, Pale Moon'.

Please describe a typical day.
I have a fairly scheduled week, but each day varies. I really do all this every day, even on the weekends, I don't take days off. Depending on the day, I might I volunteer with a food pantry, play the piano at a nursing

home/rehab centre, or work on a committee or arts guild – I belong to a several. That takes up anywhere from one to three hours, occasionally all day.

I spend anywhere from three to six hours making pottery, prepping for classes, or collecting/processing materials and/or weaving. I also spend a minimum of two hours a day (but usually much more) tending to my Etsy shops: taking photos, listing items, customer service, shipping and the like.

I also have children still at home, so there is a lot of the standard meal prep and other housework.

About six to eight times per year, I pack up the car and drive to some other place to teach basketry, for anywhere from a day to ten days. I also teach 'How to Etsy' at the local Small Business Centre/Community College, in the evening, about four times per year.

Beginning in October, until about a week before Christmas, I am literally up until 2am every single night, working on my aluminum ornaments. I don't drop any of my other outside commitments during that time, so that is when I stop making and listing new work in all my other Etsy shops.

What traditional 'heritage' methods do you use in your craft?
Different basketry methods, mostly coiling.

How have you adapted heritage or historic methods for the modern day?
These crafts were traditional because they were necessary, not because they were fun. We needed containers for daily use and, without plastic, we made them, using what was at hand. This tradition goes back a long way, predating the 'settled life' of humans. In 1995 findings of woven bits in the Czech Republic were dated about 27,000 years old. There was a reason early man was developing weaving skills. They were using what

was available, to make what was needed. This turned into our basketry tradition and is our weaving heritage.

In the current world, many people are perfectly happy using plastic and even paper bags and other manufactured items. There are some pockets where the basketry tradition remains – for instance, no one has ever found a lighter, stronger method of making a hot air balloon basket, they are using woven ones to this day! But most containers nowadays are made of something other than a weaving technique. That said, there has not yet been a machine made that can weave a basket. Every woven basket is still made by hand, so the techniques are not obsolete – yet.

Here, in our technological world, we have adapted our weaving heritage for use in hobbies and in art. That is how they have survived. There has been a renewed interested in primitive skills, and people have more leisure time, to fill with hobbies. So it is smart to adapt our useful weaving heritage to fill the 'down' time, and bring joy to people. The alternative is to lose it altogether. Not only is it fun, and beautiful, it helps people keep in touch with our collective past, and brings out the inner primitive in all of us.

So, to teach these skills to people who are looking to have fun, I have to let them start in the middle and have immediate successes. If I were an indigenous basket maker, my potential apprentices would watch me, perhaps for years, without verbal instruction, expected to observe and learn by observation alone. The actual task of weaving would be allowed only after the new learner was capable of collecting and processing their own materials, and the teacher felt they were ready. When it takes hours or days to collect and process, the materials are very precious, and not to be wasted. So a certain amount of respect and understanding is necessary before a beginner would be allowed to attempt the task.

But my students today will not sit and watch me for hours, weeks, etc. Most of them do not want to search for a longleaf pine tree (harder and harder to find), collect needles, sort them, etc. They want to MAKE

A BASKET! And so, that is what we do. Only after they have been successful, do they want to learn from the beginning. And pine needle coiling, compared with other forms of weaving, with other materials, is a very simple thing. Compare it to ash splint basketry, where one must find an appropriate ash tree (in an environment where they are disappearing daily, due to the Emerald Ash Borer,) cut it, and then pound it with a sledge hammer to get the individual rings to separate before they can be trimmed to size and only THEN be woven.

I also do not teach my students to weave 'from nothing' using only the natural material – we give them jump starts, made from things like wood or pottery to make the starting of the basket easier. We also use the tools like scissors and large-eyed sewing needles in order to make the technique easier. But these have been used for hundreds of years, in adapting coiling. Many indigenous people still use an awl to pierce a coil, and feed a piece of grass or other binder through without having it attached to a needle, that sort of thing. It is much more difficult than using a sewing needle.

So we make things easy and fun. And we make things attractive, by making art pieces that people can relate to and exhibiting them. When someone is moved by an art piece, the way is paved for them to care more about the subject of the artwork, and PERHAPS the method used to create it. Many people come to this craft by seeing pieces created by others that are just breathtakingly beautiful, or exceptionally graceful, or just appealing in a very base, visceral way that they cannot explain. Need I say how important this is? If no one cares, there is nothing to stop terminal atrophy.

About me:
I have been weaving for about twenty years and am a nationally-recognised fibre artist and teacher in the basketry arena. I have been a NICHE awards finalist and was selected by the World Craft Council

(a division of UNESCO) to represent the US as a fine craftsman on their debut website. Many people credit now-obsolete website, The Pine Needle Group, with a US resurgence in interest in the technique of coiling. I have been on the board of directors for the North Carolina Basketmaker's Association (the largest basketry guild in the USA) for sixteen years, in various capacities, including that of Convention Coordinator. I have also served several times in the National Basketry Organizations' guild committees. I am a Road Scholar instructor and teach basketry at various venues throughout the US.

Website: PamelaZimmerman.net

Email: basketsbypamela@gmail.com

Etsy shops:

BasketsByPamela.etsy.com

MakeABasket.etsy.com

PurpleToedGypsy.etsy.com

Hobbitware.etsy.com

Oakweaver – Mary Ann and Bill

What first attracted you to your craft?

I have always been drawn to baskets and the first time I saw an antique split oak basket I knew it was something I wanted to explore making. I can honestly say that I had no idea of the time and work involved, but it has been a wonderful journey.

Can you describe your journey into your craft? How did you get started? For example, do you have particular training or qualifications, or are you self-taught?

My husband and I spent many weekends visiting festivals and historic events trying to find someone who would teach us to make split oak baskets with no success until we met an incredible man who took us under his wing and worked with us to learn this beautiful craft. The Alabama Council on the Arts recognised the importance of keeping these traditional arts alive and gave us an apprenticeship grant for two years to work with Mr Jesse (Thomason). We travelled with him to many events to promote the art of split oak basket making and cherished every minute of it. He taught us how to select the right tree for splitting and how to do the actual splitting and scraping of the wood. We were fortunate that he knew how to make many of the traditional styles of oak baskets such as the fish trap and the egg basket which can require up to 100 hours to make.

Do you have any inspirations or influences? This could include particular artisans, periods in history etc.
Bill and I have continued to learn from as many basket makers as we have time for and have studied other types of basketry such as river cane, willow and various barks. Of all the basket makers we have worked with, I would have to say that Leona Waddell is the one whose work I aspire to make.

What do you enjoy most about working with the materials that you choose to work with?
We have always enjoyed the process of making something as much as the finished product, so split oak basket making is a perfect fit for us. Being out in the woods and looking for that perfect tree is a special time. There is just a feeling of being connected with all the weavers before you when you're working the oak.

Please describe the tools of your craft, and how you use them.
I guess Bill and I are mavericks when it comes to splitting oak as we don't use a froe as most do. We were taught to do our splitting with a sturdy butcher knife and that is how we've continued to do it. We use a large mallet and wedges to do the initial split and move to the butcher

knife and a smaller mallet as we progress. We also use a scraping knife to smooth up the splits as well as a drawhorse and drawknife to thin down the splits and to make the handles and rims. It's always a good idea to keep a leather guard on your knee for protection as well.

Describe your business. What items do you make? Do you sell items – if so, what? Do you teach courses? Describe the thing you have made that has made you most proud.

Bill and I spent sixteen years demonstrating as the resident basket makers at Tannehill Historical State Park and did sell our baskets there, but at the present we do more teaching and only make baskets for special orders. We teach at the John C. Campbell Folk School, Arrowmont, the Alabama Folk School and have taught at the NBO Conference in Kentucky. Honestly, the thing that has made us most proud is making new basket makers to hopefully carry on this beautiful tradition.

Please describe a typical day.

A typical day would depend on the stage in the basket making process we are at. For instance, one day we were splitting out blanks for our class at NBO. On another day we might be out in the woods searching for a tree. Once Bill gets the tree split, I will begin the actual basket making.

What traditional 'heritage' methods do you use in your craft?

We use a lot of the same tools that have been used for generations to make the split oak baskets and of course the weaving methods haven't changed.

How have you adapted heritage or historic methods for the modern day?

Although we try to keep our craft as authentic as possible there are always new methods and tools that are very helpful. For instance, instead of using scrap pieces of oak to tie the rims on before lashing, we now use clips. We will sometimes also use metal wedges in place of wooden ones. Although the wooden ones are traditional, we find that many students lack the strength to use them and the metal wedges makes it much better for them.

What advice would you give someone starting out in your field?
Find a mentor who is willing to spend time and work with you. Split oak basket making is not a craft that is easily mastered and a mentor was invaluable to us as we started out. And I would say to realise that taking a tree down to a basket is not an easy task, but with work and determination anyone can master this amazing skill.

Please add anything else you would like to tell us about, that we haven't thought of – probably a lot!
I would say to anyone who wants to learn this or any other craft to search for classes and teachers. They are out there all across the nation in many places both large and small.

About us:
Bill and I began making split oak baskets nearly thirty years ago and our focus has always been on traditional forms. We spent many years learning from Mr. Jesse Thomason in Blount County Alabama. We spent sixteen years as the resident basket makers at Tannehill State Park near Birmingham, Alabama. Our true love is teaching this beautiful craft to others in the hope of keeping it alive. We make all of our baskets from raw materials (white oak trees) and do the entire process with only hand tools. We have taught at various places over the years and also host a gathering of split oak basket makers at our home annually.
Website: oakweaver.weebly.com
Email: oakweaver@bellsouth.net

Cael Chappell, Basket Maker

What first attracted you to your craft?

I grew up in a home where my mom was always doing handcrafts (and she still does today). I always appreciated handcrafts because I saw how long and how much effort and creativity went into each item my mom made. She has been doing beadwork for more than forty years and first taught me peyote stitch when I was five years old. My dad was a woodworker, so I was also exposed at a young age to him working in his shop and creating things of beauty and function.

At 19 I started working at an African art gallery and loved the hand-carved stone sculpture from Zimbabwe. They started sending me to Africa and I was exposed to people, cultures, art, and crafts like never before. In 2002 I started my own fair trade verified company to provide economic opportunities to rural people in Africa. I was drawn to the variety and quality of basket work done throughout Africa, so I founded Baskets of Africa.

Now, every day, I'm surrounded by beautiful baskets from all over Africa and every time I go to Africa to visit with the weavers, they say 'come sit with us and weave' or 'come and make a basket with us'. For fifteen years my standard response was 'I don't have the skill or patience to make a basket.'

In 2017 that changed. I was vending African baskets at the Fiber Arts Fiesta in Albuquerque, NM where I live. One of my customers, Claire, excitedly told me she had won Best of Show in small hand weaving. I went over to see her piece and it was an abstract coiled form from waxed linen thread. I instantly recognised the coil weaving and told Claire, 'Someday I'd love to learn to weave baskets.' She quickly offered, 'I'll teach you!', and I was off and running. We met once a week for an hour and she would show me basic coiling and twining. She made it clear from the start that she had never woven a basket or anything with a pattern before – the two things I was interested in learning. But I was able to use what she taught me to coil and twine baskets. I enjoy twining more than coiling, so I focused for a year on trying to figure out what patterns I could make.

I started looking at books and the internet to find my favourite basket weavers and was really amazed at the variety and creativity I saw. In late July 2018, I attended Haystack Mountain School of Crafts for a week-long class taught by one of my favourite basket weavers in the United States, Lois Russell. On the first day I learned that I had been reverse twining rather than twining and to this day I still prefer to reverse twine and use that technique on most of my baskets.

Can you describe your journey into your craft? How did you get started? For example, do you have particular training or qualifications, or are you self-taught?
I don't have any particular training or qualifications beyond what another basket weaver once told me, 'you come from baskets'. I've immersed myself in African baskets since 2002 and I'm constantly assessing quality, patterns, colours, designs and materials of baskets.

Do you have any inspirations or influences? This could include particular artisans, periods in history etc.
I'm inspired by other weavers, whether in Africa or in the United States. I'm constantly amazed if I look at a basket and can't figure out how the weaver made some specific portion of the pattern, or how they made a shape so perfectly. I'm in constant awe as to the patience and creativity of other basket weavers. I feel as though I'm on a lifelong journey now to learn about baskets and techniques.

My favourite weaver is Lois Russell, I love her use of colour and innovative techniques.

What do you enjoy most about working with the materials that you choose to work with?

I love the tactile feel of the waxed linen. It leaves your fingers a little sticky and when you weave, the threads stay where you put them. The colours are also fantastic, I'm drawn to their deep vibrancy. I also like miniatures and small things. I love making small baskets – to put so much time and effort into making such a small item. Each basket feels like a jewel to me. I also love the portability of the waxed linen. I can weave pretty much any time and anywhere using this material.

Please describe the tools of your craft, and how you use them.

I use a small pair of scissors, sometimes a pair of tweezers and a packing tool. The scissors are to cut the threads from the spools, tweezers for tight spots to pull the woven threads tight. A packing tool is a small metal point that is used for pushing the rows down to make them tighter. When you pack as you weave, you end up with a stiffer, stronger little basket and the patterns also benefit from taking this extra step during weaving. You can use just about anything as a packing tool – I've used a large needle, a small awl, a small flat head screwdriver – but my favourite is a tool by WeaveRite which I have modified to suit my needs.

Describe your business. What items do you make? Do you sell items – if so, what? Do you teach courses? Describe the thing you have made that has made you most proud.

I make tiny baskets the size of a dime, up to baskets a few inches by a few inches from waxed linen. I also make reed baskets for storage or flower gathering or shopping, but my first love is small baskets from waxed linen. I have started selling because I simply have too many baskets to keep. I also love to give away baskets to people that appreciate the love and labour that goes into making them.

I don't teach courses yet, I hope to some day when I retire. I'm most proud of my larger waxed linen basket which is about 4 inches by 4 inches. I started it in Lois Russell's class at Haystack and worked on it for three more months, for an hour or two a day until it was finished.

Please describe a typical day.
I work every day at Baskets of Africa, surrounded by baskets from hundreds of weavers in fifteen countries in Africa. When I get home, I like to sit and weave to take away the stresses of the day and be able to focus on something so personal and satisfying as basket making.

What traditional 'heritage' methods do you use in your craft?
I'm not sure on this one. I use a variety of weaving techniques but particularly enjoy twining, reverse twining, 3-rod wale, and 4-rod wale. I make my bases using simple methods used since the beginning of time and for larger baskets I like to use Hopi-style bases.

How have you adapted heritage or historic methods for the modern day?
I think just by doing baskets for fun and beauty rather than function.

What advice would you give someone starting out in your field?
My number one advice is to get a teacher or mentor. There is no substitute for hands-on learning when it comes to basket weaving. I first tried to teach myself from kits I ordered online and failed miserably. I gave up after not finishing the first kit. Once you have some foundational knowledge of basket weaving laid down by a teacher, then you can do kits to learn new skills. But I can't stress enough how much better it has been for me having a teacher rather than trying to teach myself.
Website: https://www.facebook.com/basketsofafrica/
Website: www.facebook.com/CaelChappell/

Zebia Nangoma

My name is Zebia Nangoma. I am 35 years old. I was born and live in Uganda in East Africa. I am an artist, a beading teacher and a basket weaver and this is where I find much love and interest.

What first attracted you to your crafts?

I should say that I loved weaving since I was a little child. Growing up, I went a local government school where after-school activities like music, weaving, knitting were a must. But as other students were doing it out of order, I was doing it out of passion. I need also to tell you that the weaving was passed on to me by my beloved father. He is big weaver.

How can you describe your journey into your crafts? Or how did you get started?

Well, as I mentioned above, my basket weaving is an inborn talent that I have nurtured since I was young. I got this additional training from my primary school and the rest has been history. I just think of certain designs and I create them there and then..

Do you have any inspirations or influences? This could include particular artisans, periods in history etc.

My inspirational weaver is my father, who used to weave baskets and other beautiful crafts from palm leaves, grass, banana leaves and many other materials. Another influence should be my art and crafts teacher who would never accept a substandard basket after a successful lesson. At that period we had more variety of beautiful materials than now, so that also favoured me.

What do you enjoy most about working with the materials that you choose to work with?

I mostly use banana fibres from a banana tree which is the staple food in Uganda. The banana fibres are covers to the banana tree so when they are dry, they fall off and I harvest them for my weaving. I use the coiling method. One reason I love to use banana fibres is that they are naturally designed in black and brown colour.

Please describe the tools of your craft, and how you use them.
Talking about the tools of craft and how I use them. Well, I use a sharpened hard wire to create holes in the basket while doing the coiling. And I get the banana fibres piece to do the wrappings for the coiling. It's a little tricky to explain.

Describe your business. What items do you make? Do you sell items – if so, what? Do you teach courses? Describe the thing you have made that has made you most proud.
For my business I have a plan of opening up a craft shop because I weave different baskets using different materials. So, I am saving money to rent space for this. I also teach and already have some women that have approached me and I am looking for a convenient location that favours many of them.

Please describe a typical day.
You asked me about what I think is my masterpiece and what day I had it done. This is a table top that took me almost four months to make. I have taken it to workshop for measurements for its stands. I started it late August last year and it was finished last month.

What traditional 'heritage' methods do you use in your craft?
The tradition is that in Uganda or Africa at large, it was must for every married woman to have at least one basket in her house that she had woven. Whoever didn't possess it would be considered lazy. Our ancestors knew that a woman would get some handcraft work to keep her busy.

We are creative during the day. I embrace the coiling method because it's the one that was left behind for us by our ancestors.

How have you adapted heritage or historic methods for the modern day?
I have done this by adding in detail in the ancient weaving, for example with this weaving I use brightly coloured magazine papers to do the wrappings and then coiling. Then I still use the ancient materials to teach women how to make nice baskets that they can sell and improve their wellbeing. These include palm leaves, raffia, banana fibres, millet stalks etc. Some of these ladies are very low-income earners.

What advice would you give someone starting out in your field?
I would say that you should first of all have the love and passion for what you want to start. Then you need to a patient and good learner as every craft work needs time and patience. I have a project that I embarked on six years back and up to now I am still building on it. I never lose courage.
Email: Nangomazebia@gmail.com

Emily Jernigan Baskets
What first attracted you to your craft?
My first introduction to weaving was a beading loom when I was about 8. I would spend hours drafting designs and making bracelets for everyone I knew. I eventually drifted away from this but fell back in love with weaving when I took my first basket class with Peggy Patrick when I was 17. I made a White Oak market basket with materials she had prepared and I fell in love with basket weaving immediately. It has been a long, fun and enriching process of weaving and learning ever since. I'm 35 now and hope/plan to keep weaving until I can't anymore.

Can you describe your journey into your craft? How did you get started? For example, do you have particular training or qualifications, or are you self-taught?

I took classes over the course of several years and did a lot of practising and experimenting in between. My main teachers early on were Peggy Patrick and Emma Jackson Garrett. Over the years I have also learned from Scott Gilbert, Beth Hester, Bill and Mary Smith, JoAnn Kelly Catsos, Kathey Ervin, Jackie Abrams, Jennifer Zurick, Louise Langsner, Nancy Basket, Nancy Gildersleeve and many more. I collected and read every book I could find and made sure to weave things over and over again until I knew my muscles could remember. I am a lifelong learner for sure.

I have also been teaching Basketry techniques for eight or so years now and love sharing what I know.

Do you have any inspirations or influences? This could include particular artisans, periods in history etc.

My biggest inspiration is/was Emma Jackson Garrett. She was a native Cherokee weaver who lived in Robinsville, NC. She was spunky, funny, very open about sharing her knowledge and a very talented weaver. When I saw her baskets and realised I could learn to make similar ones if I tried hard enough, that is when I really committed myself to learning the art of basketry.

Cherokee Rivercane is a big inspiration. I'm inspired by their strength and beauty, their history and heritage and the opportunity to participate in carrying on this heritage and beauty. I'm also particularly inspired by baskets made from wild harvested materials (white oak, black ash, bark, vines, etc) and the people that make them.

Website: https://www.emilyjernigan.com/

Tunde Kiss

What first attracted you to your craft?

I always admired how beautiful things can be made from a simple material like cattail, bull rush or cornhusk. Nature gives us this material from year to year and I just have to find the way how to use them.

Can you describe your journey into your craft? How did you get started?

In 2008 I went to a course in the Hungarian Heritage House in Budapest. I learnt different Hungarian handicrafts then I decided to learn more about working with cattail, cornhusk, bulrush and straw. So, I have a qualification for basketry making. I had the basics and I started to improve my knowledge.

Do you have any inspirations or influences? This could include particular artisans, periods in history, etc

I have some Hungarian artisans whose work I like a lot. For example Gizella Török makes statues from cattail, which are beautiful. I always go about open-eyed. If I see something interesting work, or shape I start to think, that can I do it from cattail or bulrush. I like to make experiments. It's interesting that almost the same techniques are used all over the world. I have been to Asia and they use rice straw and use it almost the same way, as we do.

What do you enjoy most about working with the materials that you choose to work with?

Nowadays I like to work mostly with bulrushes. I like the green colours so the products look special and I can use it different ways. I can do toys, puppets, baskets, jewellery, lampshades. In summertime we collect the materials. I have some places where I go for the cattail and bulrushes. It's good to know that I can do everything in my work from the beginning to the end.

Please describe the tools of your craft, and how to use them?

Before using bulrushes or cattail, I have to soak it, and I wrap it an old towel to keep it wet during the work. I have to use a mould. Usually they are from wood, but sometimes I use plastic or glasses. It's important that after I finish the basket, I could remove the mould. I have a special threader that I use when I need to thread the rush.

Describe your business. What items do you make? Do you sell items – if so, what? Do you teach courses? Describe the thing you have made that has made you most proud?

I make different sized baskets, woven glasses, lampshades, handbags, belt, shoes and jewellery. I like to do things that people can use, but of course I make some decorative things too, for example flowers and dolls. I sell my products on the internet and I go some festivals where I can sell them and there are some gift shops where you can find my work.

I also run courses for children or adults. I think it's important to give our knowledge to others. In our country not too many people work with cattail or bulrushes, or even know the materials. Several times I go to festivals and teach the children some handicraft methods. In 2018 the Ministry of Agriculture announced a competition about the traditional Hungarian dressing culture. The tender made it possible to design clothes and accessories that are exclusively characterised by traditional shape, material and technique. I applied to this programme successfully and the Ministry of Agriculture sponsored me to make my collection. The fashion from the nature collection are: hat, belt, handbag, backpack and shoes. They are all made from cattail. I'm also proud that most of my products are qualified. A qualified work of applied folk art is a registered item of the Museum of Applied Hungarian Folk Art in category A or B. I have a special trademark on these products.

Please describe a typical day.
I work at home and usually make a plan one day before of what I want to do. If it needs it, I soak the material. Usually I work six to eight hours, but sometimes I like to work at night. Of course, I have to do some marketing work also.

What traditional heritage methods do you use in your craft?
I learnt different traditional methods to work with. But my favourite is the pairing weave. I can vary it depending on whatever I want to do. I like that I can do different things, so it can't be boring at all.

How have you adapted heritage or historic methods for the modern day?
I keep the historic methods, but I do modern shapes or things which we were not used to; for example, handbags, belts or jewellery. I like to combine the cattail with linen, leather or minerals.

About me:
My name is Tünde Kiss. I live in Hungary in a small village called Hollóko˝. It's listed on the world heritage list by UNESCO. I'm very lucky to live there with my family. I have three children (two daughters and a son). My family like my job, they enjoy coming with me to the festivals, and my husband helps me to collect the materials. It's good to live close to nature, especially for someone working with natural materials.

I am one of the leaders of Palóc Folk Artisan Association. We organise handicraft folk programmes, courses, exhibitions and we go to different folk festivals, where we show our crafts.

I have just started to learn 'community development' in a university, because I would like to know more about how I can use my craft knowledge in a community.

I participated in numerous festivals in Hungary and was even in China, South-Korea and Switzerland in festivals.

Most of my works are qualified and have a trademark. There were some exhibitions where my products could be seen. In 2018 I made a brand to my product: tundeDesign

Website: www.tundedesign.hu

Facebook: www.facebook.com/tundeDesign

Instagram: www.instagram.com/tundeDesign

Suzie Grieve - Foraged Fibres

What first attracted you to your crafts?

The first time I wove anything was when I was living in a community in the centre of France. The land was by a river, surrounded by a forest of hazel, which I used to weave the vegetable beds. I immediately connected to the craft; after all, weaving is just another beautiful way to connect with the plants, and I love plants.

How can you describe your journey into your crafts? Or how did you get started?

When I came back to the Lake District I was very eager to carry on weaving. I searched for hazel and willow: the materials I had in my head that people made baskets from. I found that they weren't plentiful in the land that I had access to, And so the journey began, experimenting with vines, leaves, roots and sticks that grow in abundance locally.

Do you have any inspirations or influences? This could include particular artisans, periods in history etc.

Plants! It inspires me that I'm creating something from the earth that will eventually, of course, go back to the earth. All the roots, leaves, vines and twigs I come across in the forest and their amazing shapes, textures and subtle colours. I also love using plants that people often see as invasive and feel the need to get rid of, such as bindweed, brambles and dandelion, and turning them into beautiful, functional baskets.

I'm inspired by the beautiful, finely woven cedar bark basketry made by the Native Americans, but also the current wilder experimental style of weaving in Australia.

What do you enjoy most about working with the materials that you choose to work with?
The thing I enjoy most about working with wild-foraged materials is the awareness they give you of the seasons and cycles of the earth. Spring for gathering bark, Iris and other leafy things in the autumn, winter for ivy and many, many others in-between. All this makes you more aware of nature's cycles and what's going on outside, but then again often you're too busy stripping bark till 3am or tangled up in vines to do 'owt else! Using wild-crafted materials also gives balance. I enjoy the hermiting away, weaving baskets, but if I just used prepared weaving materials I'd never leave the house and lack that connection to the whole process.

Please describe the tools of your craft, and how you use them.
The tools of my craft are mostly my hands, and maybe a foot when I get a particularly rebellious vine. I also make sure to always keep a pair of secateurs and a lal saw in my bag at all times!

Describe your business. What items do you make? Do you sell items – if so, what? Do you teach courses? Describe the thing you have made that has made you most proud.
I've just begun this past year to sell my baskets, mostly online, but through markets and shops too. I would love to make baskets full time, but this is very difficult to do (but worth it, as other crafty folk will understand). The amount of time it takes to make even one little tiny basket is crazy! All of the harvesting, drying, processing and soaking before you even start the weaving... it's just finding the folk who

appreciate this! My latest project is a book on foraged fibre basketry; an ode to those beautiful, flexible and abundant plants that grow around us and how to tangle them into baskets.

Please describe a typical day.
When I'm not working in the shop, my days consist of a mix of gathering, weaving, admin and drinking lots of tea... Most of my weaving at the moment is orders, but when I have time I enjoy making more experimental and artistic weavings.

What traditional heritage methods do you use in your craft?
In the past it would have been common place for people to use whatever plants grew around them to weave with. Nothing I'm doing is new, just a little forgotten. It's mono culture everywhere. Think of all the varieties of apples and types of wheat we would have used in the past compared to that of today. It's the same with weaving. Instead of using what's around us we clear land to grow mono crops. Willow is a good example of this.

How have you adapted heritage or historic methods for the modern day?
I only use simple tools for harvesting, processing and weaving: mostly my hands and a knife. I use the same weaving techniques as folk would have used 100 or 10,000 years ago. Although, I'm sure back then they used their local beck to soak their weaving materials in as opposed to their bath.

I love that historically, in many different traditions, people would weave baskets not just to make a vessel but also as a form of art and creativity, by weaving patterns, designs and stories into their baskets.

The way I've had to adapt is caused by the lack of wild space in these times. Even 100 years ago, with a third of today's population, there would have been so much more wild space and weaving material. I think this is partly why I've turned to so called 'weeds' and invasive plants to weave with. Learning which spaces get pruned every year and trying to use what would likely go to waste anyhow. Just last week I was in my friend's woods, gathering honeysuckle they wanted removed from certain trees anyway. I will peel and sand them and they will become beautiful, twisted ivory coloured frames for my bigger baskets.

One of my favourite things to make are woven amulet pouches: necklace baskets created from barks and various leaves.

What advice would you give someone starting out in your field?
I think so much of this depends on the type of person you are and how you like to learn. For me, I've always been obsessed with plants; identifying them, eating them, using them for medicine and just generally being with them. Weaving them is just an extension of this; another way to interact and connect with the plants.

I was happy just to experiment. I didn't watch YouTube videos or even really look at many books, although I have a couple of good ones. I just spent hours walking through the woods seeing what the fibres felt like in this leaf, or that twig or root, and if I could find a way of tangling them together.

Weaving is so primitive, simple and grounding. Rhythmical repetitive patterns that are ingrained in our DNA.

I guess my advice is just to find what works for you, but don't wait for the right book or YouTube video as most weaving is just over one, under one, over one, under and so on. Now knitting, that's complicated!

A good way I found to get to know wild fibres is to experiment with cordage making. This really helps to become familiar with the different characteristics of different plant fibres, including timing of harvests, locations where plants are likely to be found, the parts of the plants that are most flexible, how to process the material, soaking times... The list goes on!

Directory of Suppliers

These suppliers can provide you with everything you need, from tools to training courses.

http://www.willowwithies.co.uk/
Growers and suppliers of a variety of Willows for Landscape and Basketry use. The plantation is based in Derbyshire and is part of the National Forest.

https://www.musgrovewillows.co.uk/
Musgrove Willows is a family run business. Founded in 1928, the farm is on the Somerset Levels - over 60 different varieties of this sustainable and environmentally friendly product.

https://www.willowgrowers.co.uk/
Situated in the heart of the Somerset levels, this supplier specialises in the growing and preparing of willow and as well as supplying exotic basket weaving materials from all around the world including basketry cane, basketry willow, chair seating cane, willow sticks, Seagrass coils and coloured weaving materials.

https://www.worldofwillow.co.uk/
This nursery supplies cuttings of over 140 varieties. Freshly harvested basketry willow for weaving in beautiful natural colours and many weaving kits and dried rods.

https://westwaleswillows.co.uk/
Located in Carmarthenshire, West Wales Willows offers online supplies of living cuttings and rods to grow your own willow for basket weaving, ornamental use and to create living structures such as arches, domes and tunnels.

https://www.yorkshirewillow.co.uk/
This producer supplies cut price willow rods (or whips), willow cuttings, and a range of living willow kits for domes, wigwams, arbours, fences/hedges and tunnels. These cover a range of 17 selected varieties including *Salix Viminalis, Salix Tortuous* (Corkscrew or Curly Willow), *Salix Alba Vitellina* (Golden Willow), *Salix Alba Chermesina* (Scarlet Willow), *Salix Purpurea* (Chou Blue), *Salix Sachalinensis* (Sekka) and *Salix Triandra* (Black Maul).

https://www.thewillowbank.com/
This supplier stocks willow of 13 varieties in 4 different lengths.

https://www.willowsnursery.co.uk/
Willows is a small plant nursery supplies willow cuttings and more.

Useful Books
Couch, Osma Palmer. *Basket Pioneering.* New York: Orange Judd Publishing Company, Inc.,1940

Rossbach, Ed. *The New Basketry.* New York: Van Nostrand Reinhold Company, 1976

Wright, Dorothy. *The Complete Guide to Basket Weaving.* New York: Drake Publishers Inc., 1972

Useful Websites
World of Willow – willow withies, tools, books etc. –http://www.worldof willow.co.uk

The Worshipful Company of Basketmakers – http://www.basketmaker sco.org/

First Nations Arts and Crafts – https://www.sa-cinn.com/weaving/

The Weaver's View – First Peoples' basketry –https://americanindian. si.edu/exhibitions/baskets/subpage.cfm?subpage=intro

Beautiful collection of traditional baskets – https://www.medicineman gallery.com/native-american-art/antique-indian-baskets

Northwest Native American Basketweavers Association – http://www.nnaba.net/

Online Museum Exhibit –http://www.burkemuseum.org/static/baskets/index.html

Interesting programme about traditional First People basketry –https://www.kcet.org/shows/tending-the-wild/episodes/weaving-community-how-native-peoples-are-rediscovering-their

Rooted, Revived, Reinvented: Basketry in America – http://americanbasketry.missouri.edu/

Autry National Center exhibition 'Art of Native American Basketry' – http://archive.secondstory.com/project/autry

Supplier of willow withies etc. – https://www.worldofwillow.co.uk/

How to weave a basket from Jon's Bushcraft – http://www.jonsbushcraft.com/basicbasket.htm

The Basketmakers' Association – http://basket makersassociation.org.uk/basket making/

Museums to visit
http://basket makersassociation.org.uk/museums/

Woven Communities: Basket making Communities in Scotland –https://wovencommunities.org/

Elizabethan costume page – http://www.elizabethancostume.net/

Historic fashion – http://www.fashion-era.com

https://www.nativehands.co.uk/2018/04/looped-cordage-netted-bags/

http://nationalbasketry.org/

Beautiful, natural and eco-friendly woven coffins – https://www.caringcoffins.com/

Basketry groups
Basket makers South West
info@cornishwillow.co.ukbasket makerssouthwest.org.uk/

Welsh Basketmakers South Wales Group
info@welshbasket makers.co.uk
www.welshbasket makers.co.uk

Cumbria Basketmakers and Seatweavers
baskets@pettmanwillow.co.uk

Scottish Basketmakers Circle
www.scottishbasket makerscircle.org

Northumbria Basketry Group
www.northumbriabasketrygroup.co.uk

Staffordshire Basketmakers
wheatcroftwillow@googlemail.com

Three Counties Creative Crafts
Myfanwy@withies24.fsnet.co.uk

Oxfordshire Basketmakers
www.oxfordshirebasket makers.com/

Hertfordshire Basketry
hertsbasketry@gmail.com
www.hertsbasketry.org.uk

Suffolk Group
bunty.ball.t21@btinternet.com

London Basketry Group
johnrpage1949@hotmail.co.uk

Middle Earth Weavers (West Midlands)
thereremouse@gmail.com